MANAGEMENT ACCOUNTANT'S
Standard Desk Reference

Management Accountant's

Standard Desk Reference

Jae K Shim, Ph.D

Professor of Accounting and Finance

California State University, Long Beach

and

CEO, Delta Consulting Company

This edition published by
Global Professional Publishing Limited
The European Innovation Centre
Fitzroy House
11 Chenies Street
London WC1E 7EY

ISBN: 978-1-906403-07-2

Typeset by Kevin O'Connor

Printed and bound in the United States by
International Book Technology

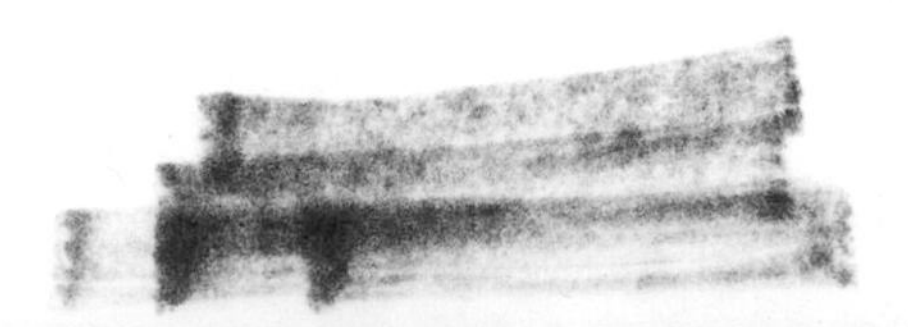

Contents

About the author

Dr. Jae K. Shim is one of the most prolific accounting and finance experts in the world. He is a professor of accounting and finance at California State University, Long Beach and CEO of Delta Consulting Company, a financial consulting and training firm. Dr. Shim received his M.B.A. and Ph.D. degrees from the University of California at Berkeley (Haas School of Business). Dr. Shim has been a consultant to commercial and nonprofit organizations for over 30 years.

Dr. Shim has more than 50 college and professional books to his credit, including, *Economic Analysis for Business and Strategic Decisions*, (Global Professional Publishing, 2008), *The International Handbook of Computer Security, Revised Edition* (Global Professional Publishing, 2007) and *Financial Management* (Barron's Business Library, 2000). Twenty-one of his publications have been translated into foreign languages, including Chinese, Spanish, Russian, Polish, Croatian, Italian, Japanese and Korean.

Dr. Shim has been frequently quoted by such media as the Los Angeles Times, Orange County Register, Business Start-ups, Personal Finance and Money Radio. Dr. Shim has also published numerous articles in professional and academic journals. He was the recipient of the Financial Management Association International's Credit Research Foundation Award for his work on cash flow forecasting and financial modeling.

Preface

The Management Accountant's Standard Desk Reference is a working guide that will assist practitioners in quickly pinpointing and solving problems. You will learn what to look for, what to do and when and how to do it. This book provides measures, guidelines, ratios, formulas, procedures, techniques and rules of thumb to provide you with solutions to virtually any managerial accounting problems—and related areas of concern—that arise. Above all, this is a practical, comprehensive desk reference.

This book is organized with ease of use in mind. It is a valuable reference tool with outlines, checklists, illustrations, step-by-step instructions, charts, sample document and other how-to information. And everything is geared to business managers and managerial accountants. It covers the managerial use of accounting, financial and operating data for planning, control and decision making. A heavy emphasis is placed on how to manage costs to be globally competitive.

Due to the nature of the subject, the book uses the multidisciplinary approach—looking at the topics from many different angles such as finance, economics, marketing, information systems, quantitative methods and the like. Heavily emphasized is the incorporation of information technology (i.e., how to use computer software) into virtually every subject covered in this book.

Furthermore, the book uses the solved problems approach, with emphasis on the practical application of managerial and cost accounting concepts, tools and methodology. The reader is provided with the following:

1. Definitions and explanations which are understandable;
2. a variety of examples illustrating the concepts and techniques which are concise;
3. ample problems and detailed suggested solutions;
4. computer software demonstration and printouts; and
5. additional materials that supplement the topic.

Keep this book within easy reach—you will find yourself referring to it often for clear, to-the-point guidance for the kind of situations you face on the job every day.

Jae K. Shim, Ph. D.

Chapter 1

Introduction to Management Accounting

Management accounting is the process of identification, measurement, accumulation, analysis, preparation, interpretation and communication of financial information, which is used by management to plan, evaluate, control and make decisions within an organization. It ensures the appropriate use of and accountability for an organization's resources.

Financial Accounting versus Management Accounting

Financial accounting is mainly concerned with the historical aspects of external reporting; that is, providing financial information to outside parties such as investors, creditors and governments agencies. To protect those outside parties from being misled, financial accounting is governed by what are called generally accepted accounting principles (GAAP).

Management accounting, on the other hand, is concerned primarily with providing information to internal managers who are charged with planning and controlling the operations of the firm and making a variety of management decisions. Due to its internal use within a company, management accounting is not subject to generally accepted accounting principles (GAAP).

The differences between financial and management accounting are summarized over the page:

Financial Accounting	Management Accounting
(1) External users of financial information	(1) Internal users of financial information
(2) Must comply with GAAP	(2) Need not comply with GAAP
(3) Must generate accurate and timely data	(3) Emphasizes relevance and flexibility of data
(4) Past orientation	(4) Future orientation
(5) Financial information	(5) Nonfinancial (e.g., speed of delivery, customer complaints) as well as financial information
(6) Looks at the business as a whole	(6) Focuses on parts as well as on the whole of a business
(7) Summary reports	(7) Detailed reports by products, departments or other segments
(8) Primarily stands by itself	(8) Draws heavily from other disciplines such as finance, economics, information systems, marketing, operations/production management and quantitative methods

The Work of Management

In general, the work that management performs can be classified as planning, coordinating, controlling and decision making. The planning function of management involves selecting long- and short-term objectives and drawing up strategic plans to achieve those objectives. In performing the coordination function, management must decide how best to put together the firm's resources in order to carry out established plans.

Controlling entails implementing a decision method and using feedback so that the firm's goals and specific strategic plans are optimally obtained. And finally, decision making is the purposeful selection from a set of alternatives in light of a given objective. Management accounting information is essential in performing all of these functions.

Cost Accounting versus Management Accounting

The difference between cost accounting and management accounting is a subtle one. The Institute of Management Accountants (IMA) defines cost accounting as: "a systematic set of procedures for recording and reporting measurements of the cost of manufacturing goods and performing services in the aggregate and in detail. It includes methods for recognizing, classifying, allocating, aggregating and reporting such costs and comparing them with standard costs."

Management accounting as defined by the IMA is the process of identification, measurement, accumulation, analysis, preparation, interpretation and communication of financial information, which is used by management to plan, evaluate and control within an organization. It ensures the appropriate use of and accountability for an organization's resources. Management accounting also relates to the preparation of financial reports for nonmanagement groups such as regulatory agencies and tax authorities. Simply stated, management accounting is the accounting used for the planning, control and decision-making activities of an organization.

From this definition of cost accounting and the IMA's definition of management accounting, one thing is clear: The major function of cost accounting is cost accumulation for inventory valuation and income determination. Management accounting, however, emphasizes the use of the financial and cost data for planning, control and decision-making purposes.

Example I

Management accounting typically does not deal with the details of how costs are accumulated and how unit costs are computed for inventory valuation and income determination. Although unit cost data are used for pricing and other managerial decisions, the method of computation itself is not a major topic of management accounting but rather for cost accounting.

The Organizational Aspect of Management Function

There are two types of authorities in the organizational structure: line and staff. Line authority is the right to give orders to subordinates. Line managers are responsible for attaining the goals set by the organization as efficiently and profitably as possible. Production and sales managers typically possess line authority.

Staff authority is the obligation to give advice, support and service to the line departments. Examples of staff authority are found in personnel, purchasing, engineering and finance. The management accounting function is usually a staff function with the responsibility for providing line managers and also other staff people with a specialized service. The service includes budgeting, controlling, pricing and special decisions.

The Controller

The chief management accountant or the chief accounting executive of an organization is called the controller (often called comptroller, especially in the government sector). The controller is in charge of the accounting department. The controller's authority is basically staff authority in that the controller's office gives advice and service to other departments. But at the same time, the controller has line authority over members of his or her department such as internal auditors, bookkeepers, budget analysts and others. (See Figure 1.1 for an organization chart of a controllership situation.)

In a large firm, the financial responsibilities are carried out by the treasurer, controller and financial vice president, often called a chief financial officer (CFO). The financial vice president is involved with financial policymaking and planning. He or she supervises all phases of financial activity and serves as the financial advisor to the board of directors.

Figure 1.1 shows an organizational chart of the finance structure within a company. Note that the controller and treasurer report to the vice president of finance. The treasurer is responsible for managing corporate assets and liabilities, planning the finances, budgeting capital, financing the business, formulating credit policy and managing the investment portfolio. The controller is basically concerned with internal matters, namely financial and cost accounting, taxes, budgeting and control functions. Figure 1.2 presents the controller's functions.

Figure 1.1: A Typical Organizational Structure

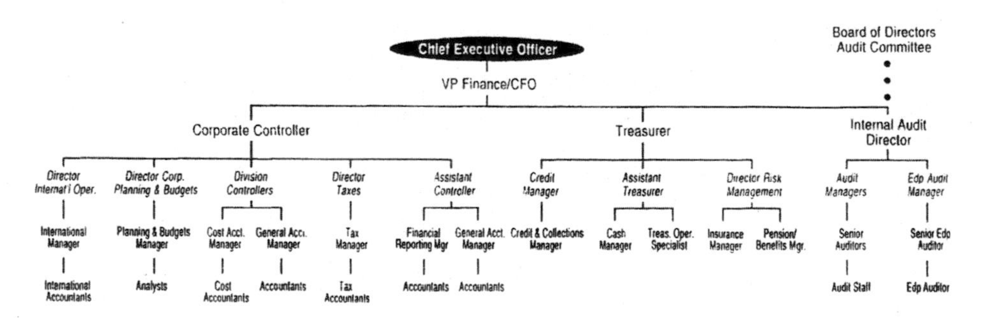

Figure 1.2: The Controller's Functions

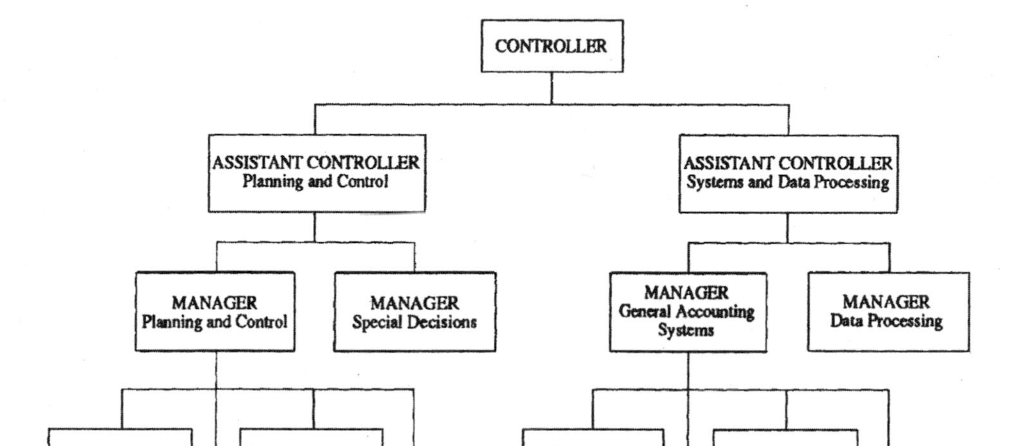

The effective, competent and timely handling of controllership and treasury functions will ensure corporate financial success. Worldwide, the actual functions and role may be slightly different, but the Financial Executive Institute, an association of corporate controllers and treasurers, distinguishes their functions as shown in Table 1.1.

It is important to note that there is no universally accepted, precise distinction between the two jobs and the functions may differ slightly between organizations because of size, personality and company policy.

Table 1.1: Functions of Controller and Treasurer

Controller	Treasurer
Accounting	Obtaining financing
Reporting of financial information	Banking relationship
Custody of records	Investment of funds
Interpretation of financial data	Investor relations
Budgeting	Cash management
Controlling operations	Insuring assets
Appraisal of results and making recommendations	Fostering relationship with creditors and investors

Table 1.1: Functions of Controller and Treasurer *(continued)*

Controller	Treasurer
Preparation of taxes	Credit appraisal and collecting funds
Managing assets	Deciding on the financing mix
Internal auditing	Dividend disbursement
Protection of assets	Pension management
Reporting to the government	
Payroll	

Government agencies and professional accounting associations worldwide have established standards in cost accounting. While the specific standards may be different in the United Kingdom from those promulgated in the United States, the standards are typically concerned with definitions, uniformity and consistency in cost accounting practices. A list of typical standards is presented below. The standards are classified into the following three categories:

1. Standards addressing overall cost accounting matters:
   400 Definitions
   401 Cost accounting standard—consistency in estimating, accumulating and reporting costs
   402 Cost accounting standard—consistency in allocating costs incurred for the same purpose
   405 Accounting for unallowable costs
   406 Cost accounting standard—cost accounting period
2. Standards addressing classes, categories or elements of cost:
   404 Capitalization of tangible assets
   407 Use of standard costs for direct material and direct labor
   408 Accounting for costs of compensated personal absence
   409 Depreciation of tangible capital assets
   411 Accounting for acquisition costs of material
   412 Composition and measurement of pension cost
   413 Adjustment and allocation of pension cost
   414 Cost of money as an element of the cost of facilities capital
   415 Accounting for the cost of deferred compensation
   416 Accounting for insurance costs
   417 Cost of money as an element of the cost of capital assets under construction
3. Standards addressing allocation of costs:
   403 Allocation of home office expenses to segments
   410 Allocation of business unit general and administrative expenses to final objectives

418 Allocation of direct and indirect costs
420 Accounting for independent research and development and bid and proposal costs

Managerial Accounting in the New Production Environment

Over the years, new technologies and management philosophies have changed the face of managerial accounting. Following are the key developments that have reshaped the discipline. We will discuss these at length in future chapters. For example, where automation and computer-assisted manufacturing methods have replaced the workforce, labor costs have shrunk from between 30 percent and 50 percent of product and service costs to around 5 percent. Managerial accounting is a major part of an active effort to improve productivity through automation, improve quality through total quality management (TQM), continuous improvement (CI), business process reengineering (BPR) and theory of constraints (TOC). Brief overviews of these now established practices are discussed below.

Total Quality Management (TQM) and Quality Costs

In order to be globally competitive in today's world-class environment, firms place an increased emphasis on quality and productivity. Total quality management (TQM) is an effort in this direction. Simply put, it is a system for creating competitive advantage by focusing the organization on what is important to the customer.

Total quality management can be broken down into:

- Total—that the whole organization is involved and understands that customer satisfaction is everyone's job.
- Quality—that everyone recognizes the extent to which products and services satisfy the requirements of internal and external customers.
- Management—there is the leadership, infrastructure and resources that support employees as they meet the needs of those customers.

Market share for many firms has eroded because international companies have been able to sell higher-quality products at lower prices. Under TQM, performance measures are likely to include product reliability and service delivery, as well as such traditional measures as profitability. In order to be competitive, firms have placed an increased emphasis on quality and productivity in order to:

1. Produce savings such as reducing rework costs.
2. Improve product quality.

Quality costs are classified into three broad categories: prevention, appraisal and failure costs. Quality cost reports can be used to point out the strengths and weaknesses of a quality system. Improvement teams can use them to describe the monetary benefits and ramifications of proposed changes.

Continuous Improvement (CI) and Benchmarking

Continuous improvement (CI), based on a Japanese concept called Kaizen, is a management philosophy that seeks endless pursuit of improvement of machinery, materials, labor utilization and production methods through application of suggestions and ideas of team members. The CI utilizes many different approaches, including: statistical process control (SPC) using traditional statistical control charts and benchmarking examining excellent performers outside the industry and seeing how you can use their best practices. Benchmarking typically involves the following steps:

1. Identify those practices needing improvement.
2. Identify a company that is the world leader in performing the process.
3. Interview the managers of the company and analyze data obtained.

Continuous improvement and benchmarking are often called the race with no finish because managers and employees are not satisfied with a particular performance level but seek ongoing improvement.

Business Process Reengineering (BPR)

TQM seeks evolutionary changes in the processes while the practice called business process reengineering (BPR) seeks to make revolutionary changes. BPR does this by taking a fresh look at what the firm is trying to do in all its processes, and then eliminating nonvalue-added steps and streamlining the remaining ones to achieve the desired outcome.

Corporate Balanced Scorecard

A problem with just assessing performance with financial measures like profit, return on investment (ROI) and economic value added (EVA) is that the financial measures are backward looking. In other words, today's financial measures tell you about the accomplishments and failures of the past. An approach to performance measurement that also focuses on what managers are doing today to create future shareholder value is the balanced scorecard. Thus the past and the future are balanced to understand and implement the most competitive and productive corporate environment.

Theory of Constraints (TOC) and Bottlenecks Management

The theory of constraints (TOC) views a business as a linked sequence of processes that transforms inputs into salable outputs, like a chain. To improve the strength of the chain, a TOC company identifies the weakest link, which is the constraint. TOC exploits constraints so that process is maximized, and where inventories and operating costs are minimized. It then develops a specific approach to manage constraints to support the objective of continuous improvement.

Bottlenecks occur whenever demand (at least temporarily) exceeds capacity. For example, although a legal secretary has enough total time to do all her wordprocessing, she may be given several jobs in quick succession, so that a queue (waiting line) builds up. This is a bottleneck, which delays the other activities waiting for the wordprocessing to be finished. TOC seeks to maximize, throughput as the phrase is called, by

1. Larger lot sizes at bottleneck work stations, to avoid time lost on changeovers;
2. small transfer batches—forwarding a small batch of work to the next work station, so that the next operation can begin before the entire lot is finished at the preceding work station; and
3. rules for inserting buffer stock before or after certain bottlenecks.

Summary

Managerial accounting is the accumulation and analysis of cost data to provide information for external reporting, for internal planning and control of an organization's operations, and for short-term and long-term decisions. This chapter outlined both the what and why of management accounting and the relationship between management accounting and its closely related fields—cost accounting and financial accounting.

The chapter also covered the discussion on the role of the controller and his role in management accounting. Because management accounting is expanding rapidly in scope, it is highly invested in total quality control and continuous improvement processes. Management accountants provide corporate officers with the information needed to improve quality and sustain productivity in a competitive environment.

Chapter 2

Cost Classification and Profit Concepts

In financial accounting, the term cost is defined as a measurement, in monetary terms, of the amount of resources used for some purpose. In management accounting, the term cost is used in many different ways. That is, there are different types of costs used for different purposes. Some costs are useful and required for inventory valuation and income determination. Some costs are useful for planning, budgeting and cost control. Still others are useful for making short-term and long-term decisions. A profit concept, contribution margin, which is extremely useful to managers, is also introduced.

Costs can be classified into various categories, according to:

1. Their management functions:
    a. manufacturing costs
        - direct materials
        - direct labor
        - factory overhead
    b. non-manufacturing (operating) costs
        - selling costs
        - general and administrative costs
        - research and development costs
2. Their timing of charges against sales revenue:
    a. product costs
    b. period costs

3. Their ease of traceability:
    a. direct costs
    b. Indirect costs
4. Their behavior in accordance with changes in activity:
    a. variable costs
    b. fixed costs
    c. mixed (semi-variable) costs
5. Their degree of averaging:
    a. total costs
    b. unit (average) costs
6. Their relevance to planning, control and decision making:
    a. sunk costs
    b. incremental costs
    c. relevant costs
    d. out-of-pocket costs
    e. opportunity costs
    f. controllable and non-controllable costs
    g. standard costs

Costs by Management Function

In a manufacturing firm, costs are divided into two major categories by the functional activities they are associated with: manufacturing costs and non-manufacturing costs, also called operating expenses.

Manufacturing Costs

Manufacturing costs are those costs associated with the manufacturing activities of the company and are subdivided into three categories: direct materials, direct labor and factory overhead. Direct materials (also called raw materials) are all materials that become an integral part of the finished product. Examples are the steel used to make an automobile and the wood to make furniture. Glues, nails and other minor items are called indirect materials (or supplies) and are classified as part of factory overhead, which is explained below.

Direct labor is the labor directly involved in making the product. Examples of direct labor costs are the wages of assembly workers on an assembly line and the wages of machine tool operators in a machine shop. Indirect labor, such as wages of supervisory personnel and janitors, is classified as part of factory overhead. Factory overhead can be defined as including all costs of manufacturing except direct materials and direct labor. Some of the many examples include depreciation, rent, property taxes, insurance, fringe benefits, payroll taxes, setup costs, material handling costs, waste control costs, inspection and quality costs, engineering, workmen's compensation and cost of idle time. Factory overhead is also called by such terms as manufacturing overhead, indirect manufacturing expenses, factory expense and factory burden.

Many costs overlap within their categories. For example, direct materials and direct labor when combined are called prime costs. Direct labor and factory overhead when combined are termed conversion costs (or processing costs).

Increasingly, an important category of factory overhead is that of quality costs. Quality costs are those that occur because poor quality may exist or actually does exist. These costs are significant in amount, often totaling 20 percent to 25 percent of sales. The subcategories of quality costs are prevention, appraisal and failure costs. Prevention costs are those incurred to prevent defects. Amounts spent on quality training programs, researching customer needs, quality circles and improved production equipment are considered in prevention costs. Expenditures made for prevention will minimize the costs that will be incurred for appraisal and failure. Appraisal costs are those incurred for monitoring or inspection; these costs compensate for mistakes not eliminated through prevention. Failure costs may be internal (such as scrap and rework costs and reinspection) or external (such as product returns or recalls due to quality problems, warranty costs and lost sales due to poor product performance).

Non-manufacturing Costs

Non-manufacturing costs (also called operating expenses) are subdivided into selling expenses, general and administrative expenses, and research and development costs. Selling expenses (also called marketing costs) are those associated with obtaining sales and the delivery of the product. Examples are advertising and sales commissions. General and administrative expenses (G & A) include those incurred to perform general and administrative activities. Examples are executives' salaries and legal expenses. Research and development costs include all costs of developing new products and services. Such costs are becoming increasingly critical as more high-technology companies enter the economy and as global competition intensifies. Many other examples of costs by management function and their relationships are found in Figure 2.1.

Product Costs and Period Costs

By their timing of charges against revenue or by whether they are inventoriable, costs are classified into: product costs and period costs.

Product costs are inventoriable costs, identified as part of inventory on hand. They are treated as an asset until the goods to which they are assigned are then sold. At that time they become the expense, i.e., cost of goods sold. All manufacturing costs are product costs.

GAAP and income tax regulations require that firms treat all manufacturing costs as product costs for external financial reporting using full absorption costing (also called absorption costing). Using full absorption costing, the firm assigns a unit's variable manufacturing cost plus a share of fixed manufacturing costs to each unit produced. Thus the total of units manufactured fully absorbs manufacturing costs. (The variable-fixed classification of costs is explained later).

Period costs are all expired costs that are not necessary for production and hence are charged against sales revenues in the period in which the revenue is earned. Firms treat all non-manufacturing costs—selling, general and administrative expenses and research/development costs—as period costs.

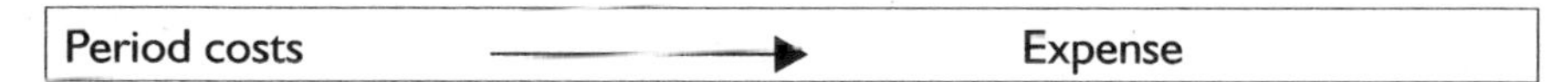

Direct Costs and Indirect Costs

Costs may be viewed as either direct or indirect in terms of the extent that they are traceable to a particular cost object. A cost object is any item for which the manager wishes to measure cost. Jobs, product lines, departments, divisions, sales territories or units produced are typical cost objects. Direct costs can be traceable to the costing object. For example, if the object of costing under consideration is a product line, then the materials and labor involved in the manufacture of the line would both be direct costs.

Factory overhead items are all indirect costs since they are not directly identifiable to any particular product line. Costs shared by different departments, products or jobs, called common costs or joint costs, are also indirect costs. National advertising that benefits more than one product and sales territory is an example of an indirect cost. Accountants may allocate them on some arbitrary basis to specific products or departments.

An Important Reminder

The following examples illustrate a cost object and its related direct costs for non-manufacturing firms:

- In a retail firm, such as a department store, costs can be traced to a department. For example, the direct costs of the shoe department include the costs of shoes and the wages of employees working in that department. Indirect costs include the costs of utilities, insurance, property taxes, storage and handling.
- In a service organization, such as an accounting firm, costs can be traced to a specific service, such as tax return preparation. Direct costs for tax return preparation services include the costs of tax return forms, database providers, computer usage and labor to prepare the return. Indirect costs include the costs of office rental, utilities, secretarial labor, telephone expenses and depreciation of office furniture.

Figure 2.1: Costs by Management Function

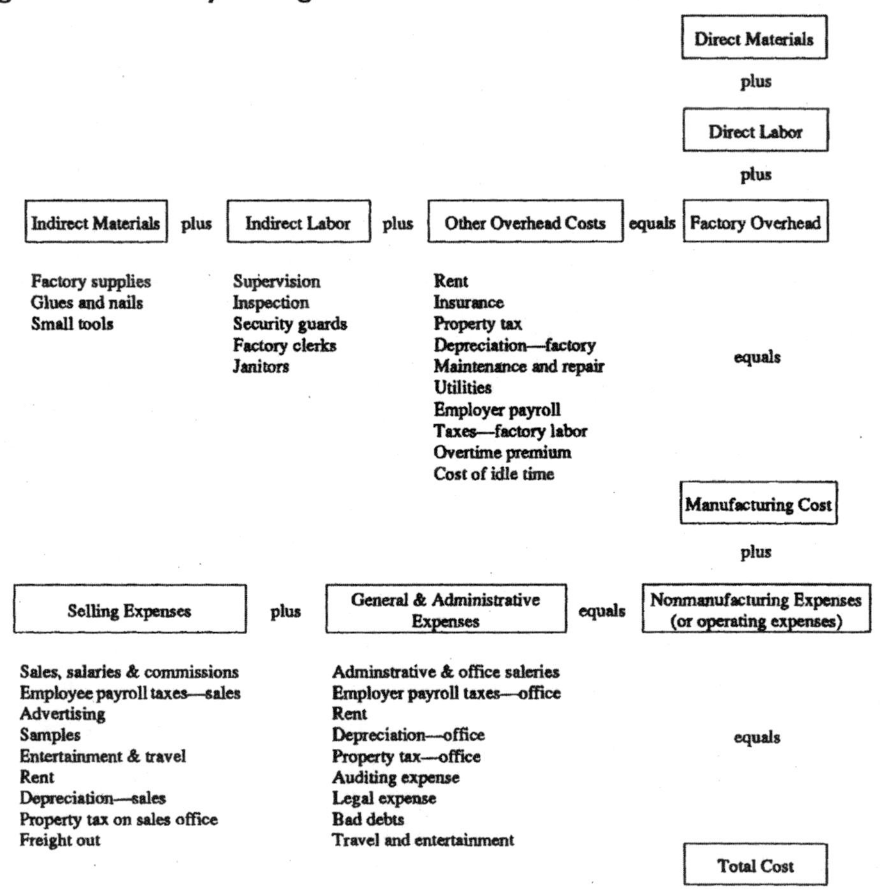

Figure 2.2: Various Classifications of Costs

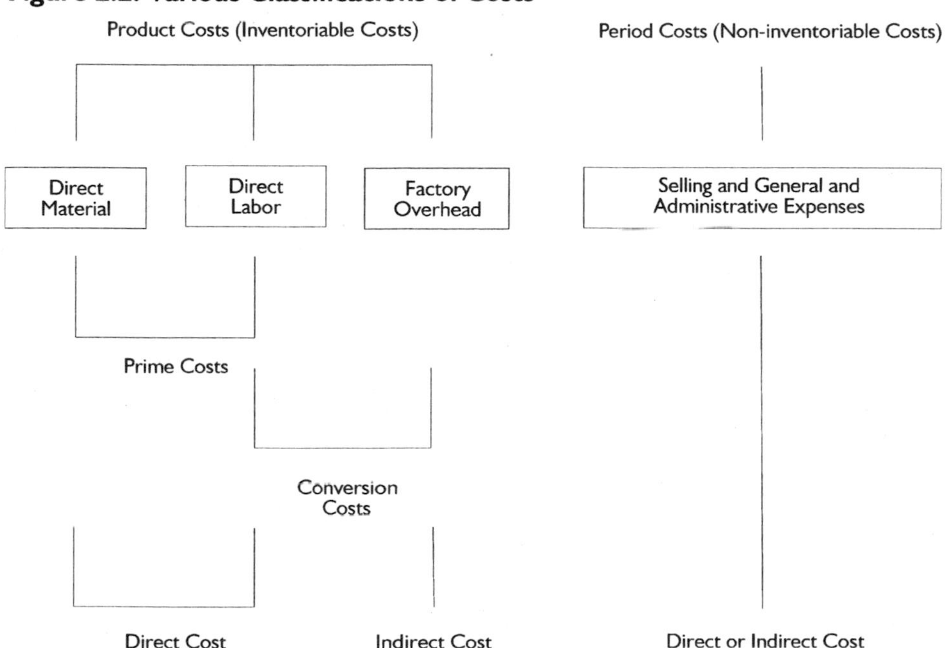

Variable Costs, Fixed Costs and Mixed Costs

From a planning and control standpoint, perhaps the most important way to classify costs is by how they behave in accordance with changes in volume or some measure of activity. By behavior, costs can be classified into the following three basic categories:

- Variable costs are those that vary in total in direct proportion to changes in activity. Examples are direct materials and gasoline expense based on mileage driven.
- Fixed costs are items that remain constant in total regardless of changes in activity. Examples are rent, insurance and taxes.
- Mixed (or semi-variable) costs are those that vary with changes in volume but, unlike variable costs, do not vary in direct proportion. In other words, these costs contain both a variable component and a fixed component. Examples are the rental of a delivery truck, where a fixed rental fee plus a variable charge based on mileage is made. Another example is power, where the expense consists of a fixed amount plus a variable charge based on consumption.

Costs by behavior will be examined in a later chapter. The breakdown of costs into their variable components and their fixed components is important in many areas of management accounting, such as flexible budgeting, break-even analysis and short-term decision making.

Unit Costs and Total Costs

For external reporting and pricing purposes, accountants are frequently interested in determining the unit (average) cost per unit of product or service. The unit cost is simply the average cost, which is the total costs divided by the total volume in units. Alternatively, the unit cost is the sum of both the variable cost per unit and the fixed cost per unit. It is important to realize that the unit cost declines as volume increases since the total fixed costs that are constant over a range of activity are being spread over a larger number of units.

Example 1

Fixed costs are $1,000 per period and variable costs are $.10 per unit. The total and unit (average) costs at various production levels are as follows:

Volume in units	Total Fixed Costs	Total Variable Costs	Total Costs (b)+(c)	Variable Cost per unit (c)/(a)	Fixed Cost per unit (b)/(a)	Unit Average Cost (d)/(a) or
(a)	(b)	(c)	= (d)	= (e)	= (f)	(e)+(f)
1,000	$1,000	$ 100	$1,100	$.10	$1.00	$1.10
5,000	1,000	500	1,500	.10	.20	.30
10,000	1,000	1,000	2,000	.10	.10	.20

The increase in total costs and the decline in unit costs are illustrated in Figure 2.3. Also note the relationships for variable and fixed costs per unit:

	Behavior as volume changes from 5,000 to 10,000	
	Total	Per Unit
Variable cost	Change ($500 to $1,000)	No change ($.10)
Fixed cost	No change ($1,000)	Change ($.20 to $.10)

Figure 2.3: Total and Unit (Average) Costs

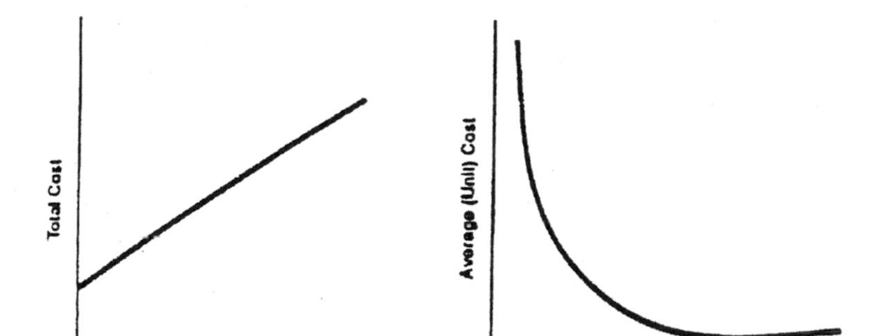

Costs for Planning, Control and Decision Making

Sunk Costs

Sunk costs are the costs of resources that have already been incurred whose total will not be affected by any decision made now or in the future. Sunk costs are considered irrelevant to future decisions since they are past or historical costs. For example, the acquisition cost of machinery is irrelevant to a decision of whether to scrap the machinery.

Example 2

Suppose you acquired an asset for $50,000 three years ago which is now listed at a book value of $20,000. The $20,000 book value is a sunk cost which does not affect a future decision.

The Incremental (Differential) Costs

The incremental cost is the difference between two or more alternatives. Incremental costs are increases or decreases in total costs, or changes in specific elements of cost (e.g., direct labor cost), that result from any variation in operations. Incremental costs will be incurred (or saved) if a decision is made to go ahead (or to stop) some activity, but not otherwise.

Example 3

Consider the two alternatives A and B whose costs are as follows:

	A	B	Difference (B - A)
Direct materials	$10,000	$10,000	$0
Direct labor	10,000	15,000	5,000

The incremental costs are simply B-A (or A - B) as shown in the last column. The incremental costs are relevant to future decisions, which will be taken up in detail in Chapter 11.

Relevant Costs

Relevant costs are expected future costs that will differ between alternatives. This concept is key to short- and long-term decisions and discussed in detail in Chapter 11.

Example 4

The incremental cost, which is the difference in costs between alternatives, is therefore relevant to the future decision. The sunk cost, which is a past and historical cost, is irrelevant to the future decision.

Out-of-pocket Costs

Out-of-pocket costs, also known as outlay costs or cash costs, are costs that require future expenditures of cash or other resources. Non-cash charges such as depreciation and amortization are not out-of-pocket costs. These are book costs. Out-of-pocket costs are usually relevant to a particular decision.

Example 5

A capital investment project requires $120,000 in cash outlays. $120,000 is an out-of-pocket cost.

Opportunity Costs

An opportunity cost is the net benefit foregone by using a resource for one purpose instead of for another. There is always an opportunity cost involved in making a choice decision. It is a cost incurred relative to the best alternative given up.

Example 6

Suppose a company has a choice of using its capacity to produce an extra 10,000 units or renting it out for $20,000. The opportunity cost of using the capacity is $20,000.

Controllable and Noncontrollable Costs

A cost is said to be controllable when the amount of the cost is assigned to the head of a department and the level of the cost is significantly under the manager's influence. For example, marketing executives control advertising costs. Noncontrollable costs are those costs not subject to influence at a given level of managerial supervision.

Example 7

All variable costs such as direct materials, direct labor and variable overhead are usually considered controllable by the department head. On the other hand, fixed costs such as depreciation of factory equipment would not be controllable by the department head, since he or she would have no power to authorize the purchase of the equipment.

Standard Costs

Standard costs are the costs established in advance to serve as goals, norms or yardsticks to be achieved and, after the fact, to determine how well those goals were met. They are based on the quantities and prices of the various inputs (e.g., direct materials, direct labor and factory overhead) needed to produce output efficiently. Standard costs can also be set for service businesses.

Example 8

The standard cost of materials per pound is obtained by multiplying standard price per pound by standard quantity per unit of output in pounds. For example, the standard price and quantity of material might be determined as follows:

Purchase price	$3.00
Freight	0.12
Receiving and handling	0.02
Less: Purchase discounts	(0.04)
Standard price per pound	$3.10

Per bill of materials in pounds	1.2	
Allowance for waste and spoilage in lbs.	0.1	
Allowance for rejects in lbs.	0.1	
Standard quantity per unit of output	1.4	lbs.

Once the price and quantity standards have been set, the standard cost of material per unit of finished goods can be computed, as follows:

1.4 pounds x $3.10 = $4.34 per unit.

Merchandising versus Manufacturing Organizations

Merchandising firms and manufacturing companies prepare income statements and balance sheets for owners, creditors and other outside parties. Both types of companies maintain levels of inventory and calculate gross margin using sales and cost of goods sold information. However, merchandising firms are less complex than manufacturing firms.

Merchandising:

- Purchase products that are ready for resale.
- Maintain only one inventory account on the balance sheet.
- Include the cost of purchases in the calculation of cost of goods sold.

Manufacturing organizations:

- Design and manufacture products for sale.
- Reflect three inventory accounts on the balance sheet.
- Determine the cost of goods manufactured to include in the calculation of cost of goods sold.

Merchandising organizations, such as Wal-Mart, Rite Aid and Office Depot, purchase products that are ready for resale. These organizations maintain one inventory account, called merchandise inventory, which reflects the costs of products held for resale. To calculate the cost of goods sold for a merchandising organization, the equation used is:

Cost of goods sold =	Beginning merchandise inventory	+	Net cost of purchases	–	Ending merchandise inventory

For example, Allison Candy Company had a balance of $3,000 in the merchandise inventory account on January 1, 20x0. During the year, the store purchased candy products totaling $23,000 (adjusted for purchase discounts, purchases returns and allowances as well as freight-in). At December 31, 20x0, the Merchandise Inventory balance was $4,500. The cost of goods sold is thus $21,500.

Cost of goods sold = $3,000 + $23,000 - $4,500 = $21,500

Manufacturing firms, such as Nokia, GM and IBM, use materials, labor and manufacturing overhead to manufacture products for sale. Materials are purchased and used in the production process. The materials inventory account shows the balance of the cost of unused materials. During the production process, the costs of manufacturing the product are accumulated in the work in process inventory account. The balance of the work in process inventory account represents the costs of unfinished product.

Once the product is complete and ready for sale, the cost of the goods manufactured is reflected in the finished goods inventory account. The balance in the finished goods inventory account is the cost of unsold completed product. When the product is sold, the manufacturing organization calculates the cost of goods sold using the following equation:

Cost of goods sold =	Beginning finished goods inventory	+	Cost of goods manufactured	-	Ending finished goods inventory

Income Statements and Balance Sheets – Manufacturer

Figure 2.4 illustrates the income statement of a manufacturer. An important characteristic of the income statement is that it is supported by a schedule of cost of goods manufactured (see Figure 2.6).

This schedule shows the specific costs (i.e., direct materials, direct labor and factory overhead) that have gone into the goods completed during the period. The two most important figures on the cost of goods manufactured statement are the total manufacturing costs and the cost of goods manufactured. Be sure not to confuse the terms total manufacturing costs and cost of goods manufactured. Total manufacturing cost includes the costs of all resources put into production during the period.

Cost of goods manufactured consists of the total costs of all goods completed during the period and includes total manufacturing cost plus the beginning work in process inventory minus the ending work in process inventory. This adjustment process is necessary because total manufacturing cost could include the goods unfinished (work in process), which need to be taken out.

Since the manufacturer carries three types of inventory (direct materials, work-in-process and finished goods) all three items must be incorporated into the computation of the cost of goods sold. These inventory accounts also appear on the balance sheet for a manufacturer, as shown in Figure 2.4.

Figure 2.4: Manufacturer's Current Asset Section of Balance Sheet

December 31, 20X0		
Current Assets:		
Cash		$ 25,000
Accounts receivable		78,000
Inventories:		
Raw materials	$ 7,800	
Work-in-process	2,000	
Finished goods	21,000	30,800
Total		$133,800

Figure 2.5: Manufacturer's Income Statement

For the Year Ended December 31, 20X0		
Sales		$460,000
Cost of goods sold:		
Beginning finished goods inventory	$ 18,000	
Add: Cost of goods manufactured (see Schedule, Figure 2.6)	261,000	
Cost of goods available for sale	$279,000	
Less: Ending finished goods inventory	(21,000)	$258,000
Gross margin		$202,000
Less: Operating expenses		
Selling and administrative expenses		(70,000)
Net Income before taxes		$132,000

Figure 2.6: Manufacturer's Schedule of Cost of Goods Manufactured

Direct materials:				
Beginning inventory	$ 23,000			
Add: Purchases	64,000			
Direct materials available for use		$87,000		
Less: Ending inventory		(7,800)		
Direct materials used			$79,200	
Direct labor			45,000	
Factory overhead:				
Indirect labor	$13,000			
Indirect material	12,000			
Factory utilities	10,500			
Factory depreciation	10,800			
Factory rent	12,000			
Miscellaneous	71,500			
			129,800	
Total manufacturing costs incurred during 20x0				$254,000
Add: Beginning work-in-process inventory				9,000
Manufacturing costs to account for				$263,000
Less: Ending work-in-process inventory				(2,000)
Cost of goods manufactured (to income statement, Figure 5)				$261,000

The Contribution Income Statement

The traditional (absorption) income statement for external reporting shows the functional classification of costs, that is, manufacturing costs vs. non-manufacturing expenses (or operating expenses). An alternative format, known as the contribution income statement, organizes the costs by behavior rather than by function. It shows the relationship of variable costs and fixed costs a given cost item is associated with, regardless of the functions.

The contribution approach to income determination provides data that are useful for managerial planning and decision making. For example, the contribution approach is useful:

(1) For break-even and cost-volume-profit analysis;

(2) in evaluating the performance of the division and its manager; and

(3) for short-term and non-routine decisions.

The contribution income statement, also known as variable or direct costing, is not acceptable, however, for income tax or external reporting purposes because it ignores fixed overhead as a product cost. The statement highlights the concept of contribution margin, which is the difference between sales and variable costs. The traditional format, on the other hand, emphasizes the concept of gross margin, which is the difference between sales and cost of goods sold.

These two concepts are independent and have nothing to do with each other. Gross margin is available to cover non-manufacturing expenses, whereas contribution margin is available to cover fixed costs. The concept of contribution margin has numerous applications for internal management, which will be taken up in Chapter 10.

A comparison is made between the traditional format and the contribution format below.

Traditional Format

Sales			$15,000
Less:	Cost of goods sold		7,000
	Gross margin		8,000
Less:	Operating expenses		
	Selling	$2,100	
	Administrative	1,500	3,600
Net income			$4,400

Contribution Format

Sales			$15,000
Less:	Variable expenses		
	Manufacturing	$4,000	
	Selling	1,600	
	Administrative	500	6,100
Contribution margin			8,900
Less: Fixed expenses			
	Manufacturing	$3,000	
	Selling	500	
	Administrative	1,000	4,500
Net income		$4,400	

Chapter Summary

Cost accounting is the accumulation and analysis of cost data to provide information for external reporting, for internal planning and control of an organization's operations, and for short-term and long-term decisions. It is important to realize that there are different costs used for different purposes. The cost/management must determine how to use cost data in order to supply the most appropriate cost information.

Cost/managerial accountants prepare the income statement in a contribution format which organizes costs by behavior rather than by the functions of manufacturing, sales and administration. The contribution income statement is widely used as an internal planning and decision-making tool.

Chapter 3

Accumulation of Costs – Job Order Costing

A cost accumulation system is a product costing system. This process accumulates manufacturing costs such as materials, labor and factory overhead and assigns them to cost objectives, such as finished goods and work-in-process. Product costing is necessary not only for inventory valuation and income determination but also for establishing the unit sales price.

We will discuss the essentials of the cost accumulation system that is used to measure the manufacturing costs of products. This is essentially a two-step process: the measurement of costs that are applicable to manufacturing operations during a given accounting period and the assignment of these costs to products.

Job Order Costing and Process Costing Compared

The distinction between job order costing and process costing centers largely around how product costing is accomplished. With job order costing, the focus is to apply costs to specific jobs, which may consist of either a single physical unit or a few like units.

Under process costing, accounting data are accumulated by the production department (or cost center) and averaged over all of the production that occurred in the department. There is mass production of like units which are manufactured on a continuous basis through a series of uniform production steps known as processes. Figure 3.1 summarizes the basic differences between these two methods.

Figure 3.1: Differences between Job Order Costing and Process Costing

		Job Order Costing	Process Costing
1.	Cost unit	Job, order or contract	Physical unit
2.	Costs are accumulated	By jobs	By departments
3.	Subsidiary record	Job cost sheet	Cost of production report
4.	Used by	Custom manufacturers	Processing industries
5.	Permits computation of	(a) A unit cost for inventory costing purposes	A unit cost to be used to compute the costs of goods completed and work in process
		(b) A profit or loss on each job	

Job Order Costing

Job order costing is the accumulation system under which costs are accumulated by jobs, contracts or orders. This costing method is appropriate when the products are manufactured in identifiable lots or batches or when the products are manufactured to customer specifications. Job order costing is widely used by custom manufacturers such as printing, aircraft and construction companies. It may also be used by service businesses such as auto repair shops and professional services. Job order costing keeps track of costs as follows: Direct material and direct labor are traced to a particular job. Costs not directly traceable – factory overhead – are applied to individual jobs using a predetermined overhead (application) rate.

Job Cost Records

A job cost sheet is used to record various production costs for work-in-process inventory. A separate cost sheet is kept for each identifiable job, accumulating the direct materials, direct labor and factory overhead assigned to that job as it moves through production. The form varies according to the needs of the company. Figure 3.2 presents the basic records or source documents used for job costing.

These include:

1. The job cost sheet. This is the key document in the system. It summarizes all of the manufacturing costs – direct materials, direct labor and applied factory overhead (to be discussed in detail later) – of producing a given job or batch of

products. One sheet is maintained for each job, and the file of job cost sheets for unfinished jobs is the subsidiary record for the work in process inventory account. When the jobs are completed and transferred, the job order sheets are transferred to a completed jobs file and the number of units and their unit costs are recorded on inventory cards supporting the finished foods inventory account.

2. The materials requisition form. This form shows the types, quantities and prices of each type of material issued for production.
3. The work ticket. It shows who worked on what job for how many hours and at what wage rate. This is also called the time ticket and illustrated in Figure 3.2.
4. The factory overhead cost sheet. It summarizes the various factory overhead costs incurred.
5. The memo for applied factory overhead. This is a memorandum that shows how the factory overhead applied rate has been developed.
6. The finished goods record. This is a record maintained for each type of product manufactured and sold. Each record contains a running record of units and costs of products received, sold and on hand.

The general flow of costs through a job cost system is shown in Figure 3.3.

Job Order Costing – An Illustration

To illustrate a job order cost system, especially the tie-in between the general ledger accounts and the subsidiary records, examine the information presented. This illustration covers the month of June, for which the beginning inventories were:

Materials inventory (material A, $10,000; material B, $6,000; and indirect materials $4,000)	$20,000
Work-in-process inventory (job No. 310; direct materials, $4,200; direct labor, $5,000; and overhead, $4,000)	13,200
Finished goods inventory (500 units of product X at a cost of $11 per unit)	5,500

Assume that job No. 310 was completed in June, and that, of the two jobs started in June (Nos. 320 and 510), only job No. 510 is incomplete at the end of June. The transactions, and the journal entries to record them, are given below:

1. Purchased $10,000 of material A and $15,000 of material B on account.

Materials inventory	25,000	
Accounts payable		25,000

To record purchase of direct materials.

2. Issued direct materials: material A to job No. 310, $1,000; to job No. 320, $8,000; to job No. 510, $2,000; material B to job No. 310, $2,000; to job No. 320, $6,000; and to job No. 510, $4,000. Indirect materials issued to all jobs, $1,000.

Work-in-process inventory	23,000	
Factory Overhead	1,000	
Material Inventory		24,000

To record direct and indirect materials issued.

Figure 3.2: Basic Records in a Job Cost System

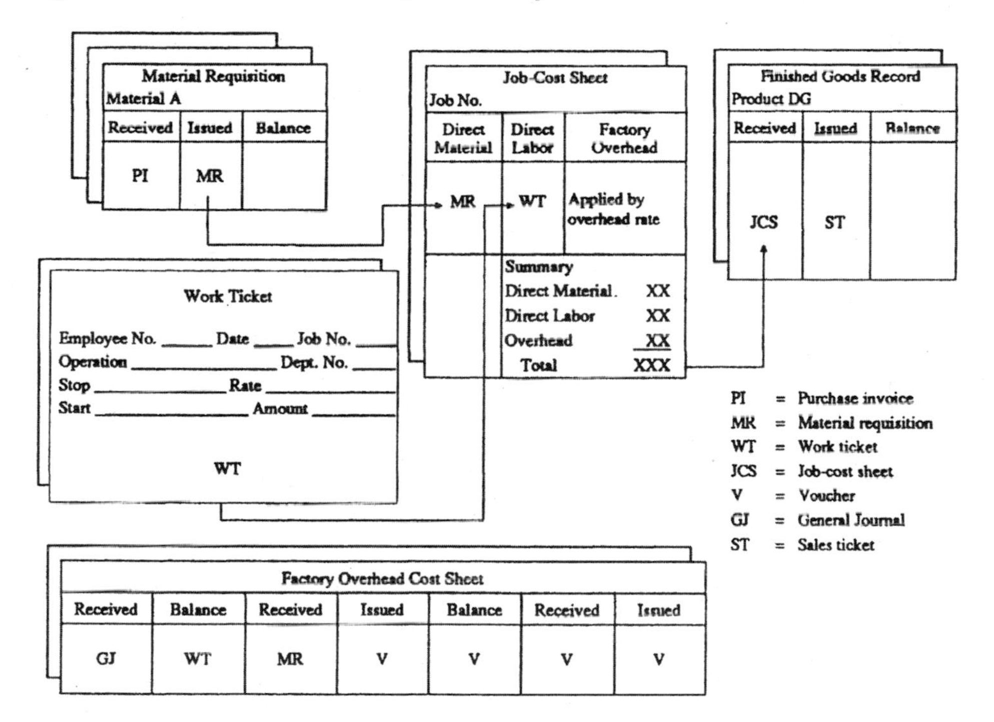

3. Factory payroll paid, $19,000.

Accrued wages payable	19,000
Cash	19,000

To record cash paid to factory employees in June.

Figure 3.3: Job Cost System – Flow Chart of Ledger Relationships

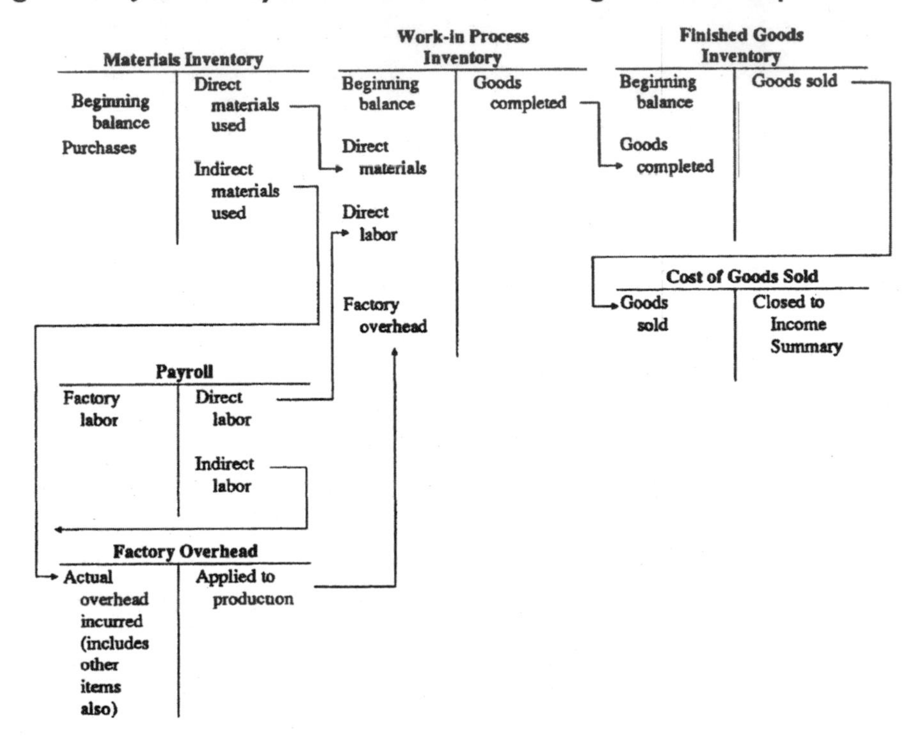

4. Payroll costs distributed: direct labor, $20,000 (job No. 310, $5,000; job No. 320, $12,000; and job No. 510, $3,000); and indirect labor, $5,000.

Work-in-process inventory	20,000	
Factory overhead	5,000	
Payroll summary		25,000

To distribute factory labor costs incurred.

5. Other factory overhead costs incurred:

Payroll taxes accrued	$3,000
Repairs (on account)	1,000
Property taxes accrued	4,000
Heat, light and power (on account)	2,000
Depreciation	5,000
	$15,000

Factory Overhead	15,000	
Accounts payable		3,000
Accrued payroll taxes		3,000
Accrued property taxes payable		4,000
Accumulated depreciation		5,000

To record factory overhead costs incurred.

6. Factory overhead applied to production (at rate of 80 percent of direct labor cost):

Job No. 310, product Y (0.80 x $5,000)	$4,000
Job No. 320, product Z (0.80 x $12,000)	9,600
Job No. 510, product W (0.80 x $3,000)	2,400
	$16,000

Work in process inventory	16,000	
Factory overhead		16,000

To record application of overhead to production.

It is important to note that as factory overhead costs are incurred, they are recorded in a subsidiary ledger and debited to the factory overhead account, as shown in journal entries nos. 2, 5 and 6.

7. The factory overhead costs applied to production are periodically credited to the factory overhead account and debited to the work-in-process account, as illustrated in journal entry no. 7). The issue of factory overhead application will be discussed in detail later in the chapter.

8. Jobs completed and transferred to finished goods inventory (see Figure 3.4 for details):

Job No. 310 (4,000 units of product Y @ $6.30)	$25,200
Job No. 320 (10,000 units of product Z @ $3.56)	35,600

Finished goods inventory	60,800	
Work in process inventory		60,800

To record completed production for June.

9. Sales on account for the month: 500 units of product X for $8,000, cost, $5,500; and 10,000 units of product Z for $62,000, cost, $35,600 (job No. 320).

Accounts receivable	70,000	
Sales		70,000

To record sales on account ($8,000 + $62,000) for June.

Cost of goods sold	41,100	
Finished goods inventory		41,100

To record cost of goods sold ($5,500 + $35,600) for June.

After the above entries have been posted to the accounts of the company, the work-in-process inventory and finished goods inventory accounts would appear (in T-account form) as follows:

Work-in-Process Inventory

June 1 balance	13,200	Completed	60,800
Direct materials used	23,000		
Direct labor cost incurred	20,000		
Overhead applied	16,000		

Finished Goods Inventory

June 1 balance	5,500	Sold	41,100
Completed	60,800		

The work-in-process inventory account has a balance at June 28 of $11,400, which agrees with the total costs charged thus far to job No. 510, as is shown in Figure 3.4. These costs consist of direct materials, $6,000; direct labor, $3,000 and factory overhead, $2,400. The finished foods inventory account has a balance at June 28 of $25,200. The finished goods inventory card for product Y supports this amount (see Figure 3.4), showing that there are indeed units of product Y on hand having a total cost of $25,200.

Note that the entries in the ledger accounts given above are often made from summaries of costs and are thus entered only at the end of the month. On the other hand, in order to keep management informed as to costs incurred, the details of the various costs incurred may be recorded more frequently, often daily.

The above example should be studied until the real advantages of using overhead rates (including predetermined rates) are clear. Three jobs were worked on during the month. Job No. 310 was started last month and completed in June.

Job No. 320 was started and completed in June. And job No. 510 was started but not finished in June. Each required different amounts of direct materials and direct labor (and, perhaps, different types of direct labor). Under these conditions, there is simply no way to apply overhead to products without the use of a rate based on some level of activity.

Also be aware that the use of a predetermined overhead rate permits the computation of unit costs of jobs No. 310 and No. 320 at the time of their completion rather than waiting until the end of the month. But this advantage is secured only at the cost of keeping more detailed records of the costs incurred. As we shall see below, the other major cost system – process costing – requires far less record keeping, but the computation of unit costs is more complex.

Example 1

Chiphard Works collects its cost data by the job order cost system. For job No. 123, the following data are available:

Direct Materials		Direct Labor	
7/14 Issued	$1,200	Week of July 20	180 hrs. @$6.50
7/20 Issued	650	Week of July 26	140 hrs. @ 7.25
7/25 Issued	350		
	$2,200		

Factory overhead is applied at the rate of $4.50 per direct labor hour.

We will compute the cost of job No. 123 and the sales price of the job, assuming that it was contracted with a markup of 40 percent of cost.

(a) The cost of job is:

Direct material		$2,200
Direct labor:		
180 hrs. x $6.50	$1,170	
140 hrs. x $7.25	1,015	2,185
Factory overhead applied:		
320 hrs. x $4.50		1,440
Cost of Job 123		$5,825

(b) The sales price of the job is:

$5,825 + 40% ($5,825) = $5,825 + $2,330 = $8,155

Figure 3.4: Job Cost Sheets and Supporting Inventory Cards

Material Requisition		
Material A		
Received	Issued	Balance
		$10,000
$10,000		20,000
	$1,000	19,000
	8,000	11,000
	2,000	9,000

Material Requisition		
Material B		
Received	Issued	Balance
		$ 6,000
$15,000		21,000
	$2,000	19,000
	6,000	13,000
	4,000	9,000

Job Cost Sheet (Product Y) Job No. 310

Date	Direct Materials	Direct Labor	Factory Overhead Applied
June	$4,200	$ 5,000	$4,000
	A 1,000	5,000	4,000
	B 2,000	$10,000	$8,000
	$7,200		
	Job completed (4,000 units of Product Y @ $6.30). Total cost, $25,200.		

Job Cost Sheet (Product Z) Job No. 320

Date	Direct Materials	Direct Labor	Factory Overhead Applied
June	A 8,000	$12,000	$9,600
	B 6,000		
	$14,000		
	Job completed (10,000 units of Product Z @ $3.56). Total cost, $35,600.		

Job Cost Sheet (Product W) Job No. 510

Date	Direct Materials	Direct Labor	Factory Overhead Applied
June	A 2,000	$3,000	$2,400
	B 4,000		
	Job completed (4,000 units of Product W). Cost to date, $11,400.		

Finished Goods Record		
Product X		
Received	Issued	Balance
		$5,500
	$5,500	-0-

Finished Goods Record		
Product Y		
Received	Issued	Balance
$25,200		$25,200

Finished Goods Record		
Product Z		
Received	Issued	Balance
$35,600		$35,600
	$35,600	-0-

Example 2

The following account appears in the ledger after only part of the postings have been completed for June:

Work-in-Process	
Balance, June	$132,200
Direct materials	134,500
Direct labor	112,000
Factory overhead	220,000

Job finished during June are summarized as follows:

Job 101	$56,700
Job 107	230,200
Job 111	127,500
	$414,400

We will prepare the journal entry to record the jobs completed and determine the cost of the unfinished jobs at June 30.

(a) The journal entry is:

Finished goods	414,400	
Work in process		414,400

(b) The cost of unfinished jobs is:
$598,700 - $414,400 = $184,300

Factory Overhead Application

Many items of factory overhead cost are incurred for the entire factory and for the entire accounting period and cannot be specifically identified with particular jobs. Furthermore, the amount of actual factory overhead costs incurred is not usually available until the end of the accounting period. But it is often critical to make cost data available for pricing purposes as each job is completed. Therefore, in order for job costs to be available on a timely basis, it is customary to apply factory overhead by using a predetermined factory overhead rate.

Although an actual rate is simple to compute, the results are misleading because overhead rates may fluctuate significantly from month to month. When these fluctuations occur, similar jobs completed in different months will have overhead costs and total costs that differ.

Predetermined Factory Overhead Rate

Regardless of the cost accumulation system used (i.e., job order or process), factory overhead is applied to a job or process. Companies use predicted levels of activity and cost rather than actual levels. The successful assignment of factory overhead costs depends on a careful estimate the total overhead costs and a good forecast of the activity used as the cost driver.

The predetermined overhead rate is determined as follows:

$$\text{Predetermined overhead rate} = \frac{\text{Budgeted annual factory overhead costs}}{\text{Budgeted annual activity units (direct labor hours, machine hours, etc.)}}$$

Budgeted activity units used in the denominator of the formula, more often called the denominator activity level or cost driver, are measured in:

(1) direct labor hours

(2) machine hours

(3) direct labor costs

(4) direct material dollars or

(5) production units.

Disposition of Under- and Over-Applied Overhead

Inevitably, actual overhead cost incurred during a period and factory overhead costs applied will differ. Conventionally, at the end of the year, the difference between actual overhead and applied overhead is immaterial. On the other hand, if a material difference exists, work-in-process, finished goods and cost of goods sold are adjusted on a proportionate basis based on units or dollars at year-end for the deviation between actual and applied overhead. Underapplied overhead and overapplied overhead results as follows:

Underapplied overhead = Applied overhead < Actual overhead

Overapplied overhead = Applied overhead > Actual overhead

Example 3

Two companies have prepared the following budgeted data for the year 20X1:

	Company X	Company Y
Predetermined rate based on	Machine hours	Direct labor cost
Budgeted overhead	$200,000 (1)	$240,000 (1)
Budgeted machine-hours	100,000 (2)	
Budgeted direct labor cost		$160,000 (2)
Predetermined overhead rate (1)/(2)	$2 per machine hour	150% of direct labor cost

Now assume that actual overhead costs and the actual level of activity for 20X1 for each firm are shown as follows:

	Company X	Company Y
Actual overhead costs	$198,000	$256,000
Actual machine hours	96,000	
Actual direct labor cost		$176,000

Note that for each company, the actual cost and activity data differ from the budgeted figures used in calculating the predetermined overhead rate. The computation of the resulting underapplied and overapplied overhead for each company is provided below:

	Company X	Company Y
Actual overhead costs	$198,000	$256,000
Factory overhead applied to work-in-process during 20X1:		
96,000 actual machine-hours x $2	192,000	
$176,000 actual direct labor cost x 150%		264,000
Underapplied (overapplied) factory overhead	$ 6,000	($ 8,000)

Plantwide Versus Departmental Overhead Rates

As the degree of aggregation increases from simply combining related cost pools to combining all factory overhead, information may become more distorted. The following provides a simple example of the differing results obtained between using a departmental and plantwide overhead rate.

Example 4

Allison Company has two departments: assembly and finishing. Assembly work is performed by robots, and a large portion of this department's overhead cost consists of depreciation and electricity charges. Finishing work is performed manually by skilled laborers, and most charges in this department are for labor, fringe benefits, indirect materials and supplies.

The company makes two products: A and B. Product A requires five machine hours in assembly and one direct labor hour in finishing; product B requires two machine hours in assembly and three direct labor hours in finishing. Figure 3.5

shows estimated overhead costs and activity measures and the computations of departmental and plantwide overhead rates. Product overhead application amounts for A and B are also given.

There is a significant difference in the overhead applied to each product using departmental versus plantwide rates. If departmental rates are used, product cost more clearly reflects the different amounts and types of machine/labor work performed on the two products. If a plantwide rate is used, essentially, each product only absorbs overhead from a single department – from assembly if machine hours are used and from finishing if direct labor hours are used. Use of a plantwide rate ignores the dissimilarity of work performed in the departments.

Figure 3.5: Plantwide versus Departmental Overhead Rates

	Assembly	Finishing	Total
Estimated annual overhead	$300,200	$99,800	$400,000
Estimated annual direct labor hours (DLH)	5,000	20,000	25,000
Estimate annual machine hours (MH)	38,000	2,000	40,000

(1)	Total plantwide overhead =	$300,200 + $99,800 = $400,000
	Plantwide overhead rate using DLH)	($400,000/25000 = $16.00)
(2)	Departmental overhead rates:	
	Assembly (automated)	$300,200/38,000 = $7.90 per MH
	Finishing (manual)	$99,800/20,000 = $4.99 per DLH

		To Product A	To Product B
(1)	Overhead assigned using plantwide rate:		
	based on DLH	1($16.00) = $16.00	3($16.00) = $48.00
(2)	Overhead assigned using departmental rates:		
	Assembly	5($7.90) = $39.50	2($7.90) = $15.80
	Finishing	1($4.99) = 4.99	3($4.99) = 14.97
	Total	$44.49	$30.77

Use of plantwide overhead rates rather than departmental rates may also contribute to problems in product pricing. While selling prices must be reflective of market conditions, management typically uses cost as a starting point for setting prices. If plantwide rates distort the true cost of a product, selling prices might be set too low or too high, causing management to make incorrect decisions.

Example 5

Assume in the case of Allison Company that direct materials and direct labor costs for product A are $5 and $35, respectively. Adding the various overhead amounts to these prime costs gives the total product cost under each method. Figure 3.6 shows these product costs and the profits or loss that would be indicated if product A has a normal market selling price of $105.

Use of the product costs developed from plantwide rates could cause Allison management to make erroneous decisions about product A. If the cost figure developed from a plantwide direct labor hour basis is used, management may think that product A is significantly more successful than it actually is. Such a decision could cause resources to be diverted from other products. If the cost containing overhead based on the plantwide machine hour allocation is used, management may believe that product A should not be produced, because it appears not to be generating a very substantial gross profit.

In either instance, assuming that machine hours and direct labor hours are the best possible allocation bases for assembly and finishing, respectively, the only cost that gives management the necessary information upon which to make resource allocation and product development/elimination decisions is the one produced by using the departmental overhead rates.

Figure 3.6: Total Product Costs and Profits

	Departmental Rates	Plantwide Rate (DLH)
Direct materials	$ 5.00	$ 5.00
Direct labor	35.00	35.00
Overhead	44.49	16.00
Total Cost	$ 84.49	$ 56.00
Selling Price	$105.00	$105.00
Gross profit (margin)	$ 20.51	$ 49.00
Profit margin	19.5%	46.7%

Example 6

A company uses a budgeted overhead rate in applying overhead to production orders on a labor-cost basis for department A and on a machine-hour basis for department B. At the beginning of the year, the company made the following predictions:

	Department A	Department B	Total
Budgeted factory overhead	$72,000	$75,000	$147,000
Budgeted direct labor cost	64,000	17,500	81,500
Budgeted machine hours	500	10,000	10,500

The predetermined overhead rates for each department are:

Department A: $72,000/$64,000	= $1.125 per labor dollar or 112.5%
Department B: $75,000/10,000	= $7.50 per machine hour

During the month of January, the cost record for a job order, No. 105, which was processed through both departments, shows the following:

	Department A	Department B	Total
Materials issued	$30	$45	$75
Direct labor cost	36	25	61
Machine hours	6	15	21

The total applied overhead for job order No. 105 follows:

Department A: $36 x 1.125	$40.50
Department B: 15 x $7.50	112.50
	$153.00

Assume job order No. 105 consisted of 30 units of product, what is the total cost and unit cost of the job?

	Department A	Department B	Total
Direct material	$30.00	$45.00	$75.00
Direct labor	36.00	25.00	61.00
Applied overhead	40.50	112.50	153.00
Total	$106.50	$182.50	$289.00

Hence, the total cost of the job is $106.50 + $182.50 = $289; the unit cost is $ 9.63 ($289/30 units).

Example 6

Refer to Example 6 and assume that the company uses a single plantwide rate based on direct labor costs. What is the total applied overhead for job order No. 105 and the total cost and unit cost of the job?

The predetermined overhead rate is:

$147,000/$81,500 = 180% of direct labor cost

Then the total applied overhead for the job is:

$61 x 180% = $109.80 (as compared to $153.00 under a department rate system)

Therefore, the total cost of the job is $245.80 ($75.00+$61.00+$109.80); the unit cost is $8.19 ($245.80/30 units). Notice the difference in the unit cost $8.19 versus $9.63.

Example 7

Refer to Example 6 and assume, at the end of the year, that actual factory overhead amounted to $80,000 in department A and $69,000 in department B. Assume further that the actual direct labor cost was $74,000 in department A and the actual machine hours were 9,000 in department B. Then, the overapplied or underapplied overhead for each department would be:

Department A:	Applied overhead (1.125 x $74,000)	$83,250
	Actual overhead	80,000
	Overapplied overhead	$ 3,250
Department B:	Applied overhead ($7.50 x 9,000)	$67,500
	Actual overhead	69,000
	Underapplied overhead	$(1,500)

Chapter Summary

Unit costs are necessary for inventory valuation, income determination, and pricing. This chapter provided an introduction to the two basic cost accumulation systems: job order costing and process costing. Job order costing was discussed in detail.

Job order costing attaches costs to specific jobs by means of cost sheets established for each job. Direct material and direct labor costs are traced to specific jobs; factory overhead costs are applied by jobs, using a predetermined overhead rate. This chapter also discussed ways in which to develop the overhead application rate. In the next chapter, we discuss process cost accounting.

Chapter 4

Activity-based Costing and Activity-based Management

Many companies use a traditional cost system such as job-order costing or process costing, or some hybrid of the two. This traditional system may provide distorted product cost information. In fact, companies selling multiple products are making critical decisions about product pricing, making bids or product mix, based on inaccurate cost data. In all likelihood, the problem is not with assigning the costs of direct labor or direct materials. These prime costs are traceable to individual products and most conventional cost systems are designed to ensure that this tracing takes place.

However, the assignment of overhead costs to individual products is another matter. Using the traditional methods of assigning overhead costs to products, using a single predetermined overhead rate based on any single activity measure, can produce distorted product costs. The growth in the automation of manufacturing (such as increased use of robotics, high-tech machinery and other computer-driven processes) has changed the nature of manufacturing and the composition of total product cost. The significance of direct labor cost has diminished and overhead costs have increased. In this environment, overhead application rates based on direct labor or any other volume-based cost driver may not provide accurate overhead charges since they no longer represent cause and effect relationships between output and overhead costs.

Activity-based costing (ABC) attempts to get around this problem. An ABC system assigns costs to products based on the product's use of activities, not product volume. It has proved to produce more accurate product costing results in an environment where there is diversity in product line and services coming out of the same shop. A recent survey by the Institute of Management Accounting shows that over 30 percent of the companies responded are using ABC systems to replace their existing traditional cost systems.

Composition of Product Cost

The continuing advances of technology and automation have produced entirely new patterns of product costs. The three elements of product cost are still direct materials, direct labor and factory (manufacturing) overhead. However, the percentage that each element contributes to the total cost of a product has changed. Prior to 1980s, direct labor was the dominant cost element, making up over 40 percent of total product cost. Direct materials contributed 35 percent and manufacturing overhead around 25 percent of total cost. Seventy-five percent of total product cost was a direct cost, traceable to the product. Improved production technology caused a dramatic shift in the three products cost elements. Labor was increasingly replaced by machines and direct labor was reduced significantly. Today, only 50 percent of the cost of a product is directly traceable to the product; the other 50 percent is manufacturing overhead, an indirect cost.

Figure 4.1: Product Cost

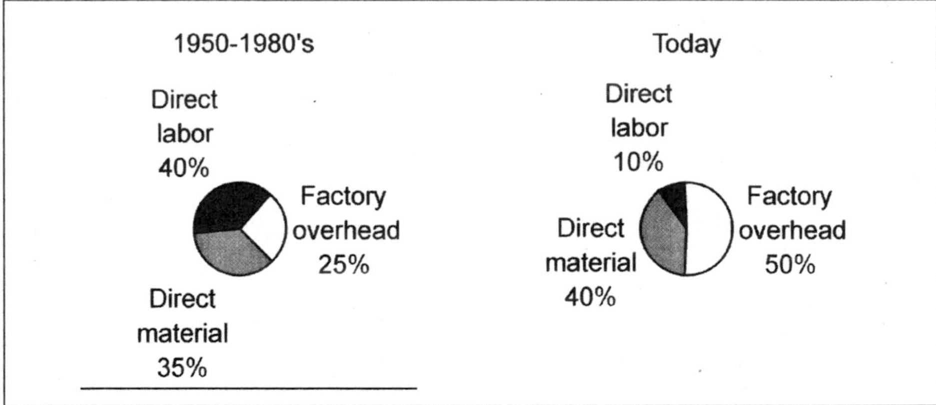

Overhead Costing: A Single-Product Situation

The accuracy of overhead cost assignment becomes an issue only when multiple products are manufactured in a single facility. If only a single product is produced, all overhead costs are caused by it and traceable to it. The overhead cost per unit is simply the total overhead for the year divided by the number of hours or units produced, which was discussed in detail in the previous chapters.

The cost calculation for a single-product setting is illustrated in Table 4.1. There is no question that the cost of manufacturing the product illustrated in Table 4.1 is $28.00 per unit. All manufacturing costs were incurred specifically to make this product. Thus, one way to ensure product-costing accuracy is to focus on producing one product. For this reason, some multiple product firms choose to dedicate entire plants to the manufacture of a single product.

By focusing on only one or two products, small manufacturers are able to calculate the cost of manufacturing the high-volume products more accurately and price them more effectively.

Table 4.1: Unit Cost Computation: Single Product

	Manufacturing Costs	Produced Units	Unit Cost
Direct materials	$800,000	50,000	$16.00
Direct labor	200,000	50,000	4.00
Factory overhead	400,000	50,000	8.00
Total	$1,400,000	50,000	$28.00

Overhead Costing: A Multiple-Product Situation

In a multiple-product or multi-job situation, manufacturing overhead costs are caused jointly by all products. The problem is one of trying to identify the amount of overhead caused or consumed by each. This is accomplished by searching for cost drivers, or activity measures that cause costs to be incurred.

In a traditional setting, it is normally assumed that overhead consumption is highly correlated with the volume of production activity, measured in terms of direct labor hours, machine hours or direct labor dollars. These volume-related cost drivers are used to assign overhead to products. Volume-related cost drivers use either plantwide or departmental rates, which was discussed in detail in the previous chapter.

Example 1

To illustrate the limitation of this traditional approach, assume that Aggie Manufacturing Company has a plant that produces two high-quality fertilizer products; Nitro-X and Nitro-Y. Product costing data are given in Table 4.2. Because the quantity of Nitro-Y produced is five times greater than that of Nitro-X, Nitro-X can be labeled a low-volume product and Nitro-Y a high-volume product.

For simplicity, only four types of factory overhead costs are assumed: setup, quality control, power and maintenance. These overhead costs are allocated to the two production departments using the direct method. Assume that the four service centers do not interact. Setup costs are allocated based on the number of production runs handled by each department. Quality control costs are allocated by the number of inspection hours used by each department. Power costs are allocated in proportion to the kilowatt hours used. Maintenance costs are allocated in proportion to the machine hours used.

Plantwide Overhead Rate

A common method of assigning overhead to products is to compute a plantwide rate, using a volume-related cost driver. This approach assumes that all overhead cost variation can be explained by one cost driver. Assume that machine hours is chosen.

Table 4.2: Product Costing Data

	Nitro-X	Nitro-Y	Total
Units produced per year	10,000	50,000	60,000
Production runs	20	30	50
Inspection hours	800	1,200	2,000
Kilowatt hours	5,000	25,000	30,000
Prime costs (direct materials and direct labor)	$50,000	$250,000	$300,000

	Departmental Data		
	Department 1	Department 2	Total
Direct labor hours:			
Nitro-X	4,000	16,000	20,000
Nitro-Y	76,000	24,000	100,000
Total	80,000	40,000	120,000
Machine hours:			
Nitro-X	4,000	6,000	10,000
Nitro-Y	16,000	34,000	50,000
Total	20,000	40,000	60,000
Overhead costs:			
Setup costs	$48,000	$48,000	$96,000
Quality control	37,000	37,000	74,000
Power	14,000	70,000	84,000
Maintenance	13,000	65,000	78,000
Total	$112,000	$220,000	$332,000

Dividing the total overhead by the total machine hours yields the following overhead rate:

Plantwide rate = $332,000/60,000 = $5.53/machine hour

Using this rate and other information from Table 4.2, the unit cost for each product can be calculated, as given in Table 4.3.

Table 4.3: Unit Cost Computation: Plantwide Rate

Nitro-X	
Prime costs	$50,000
Overhead costs $5.53 X 10,000	55,300
	$105,300
Unit cost $105,300/10,000 units	$10.53
Nitro-Y	
Prime costs	$250,000
Overhead costs $5.53 X 50,000	276,500
	$526,500
Unit cost $526,500/50,000 units	$10.53

Departmental Rates

Based on the distribution of labor hours and machine hours in Table 4.2, department 1 is labor intensive and department 2 machine oriented. Furthermore, the overhead costs of department 1 are about one half those of department 2. Based on these observations, it is obvious that departmental overhead rates would reflect the consumption of overhead better than a plantwide rate. Product costs would be more accurate using departmental rates rather than a plantwide rate.

This approach would yield the following departmental rates, using direct labor hours for department 1 and machine hours for department 2:

Department 1 rate	= $112,000/80,000
	= $1.40/labor hour
Department 2 rate	= $220,000/40,000
	= $5.50/machine hour

Using these rates and the data from Table 4.2, the computation of the unit costs for each product is shown in Table 4.4.

Table 4.4: Unit Cost Computation: Department Rates

Nitro-X	
Prime costs	$50,000
Overhead costs:	
Department 1: $1.40 X 4,000 = $ 5,600	
Department 2: $5.50 X 6,000 = 33,000	38,600
	$88,600
Unit cost $88,600/10,000 units	$8.86
Nitro-Y	
Prime costs	$250,000
Overhead costs:	
Department 1: $1.40 X 76,000 = $106,400	
Department 2: $5.50 X 34,000 = 187,000	293,400
	543,400
Unit cost $543,400/50,000 units	$10.87

Plantwide Rate versus Departmental Rates

Using a single, plantwide overhead rate based on machine hours gave the same overhead application and cost per unit for Nitro-X and Nitro-Y, i.e., $10.53. But this would not be an accurate measurement of the underlying relationship, because Nitro-X made light use of overhead incurring factors while Nitro-Y made heavy use of such services.

To summarize, when products are heterogeneous, receiving uneven attention and effort as they move through various departments, departmental rates are necessary to achieve more accurate product costs.

Problems with Costing Accuracy

The accuracy of the overhead cost assignment can be challenged regardless of whether the plantwide or departmental rates are used. The main problem with either procedure is the assumption that machine hours or direct labor hours drive cause all overhead costs.

From Table 4.2, we know that Nitro-Y—with five times the volume of Nitro-X—uses five times the machine hours and direct labor hours. Thus, if a plantwide rate is used, Nitro-Y will receive five times more overhead costs. But does it make sense? Is all overhead driven by volume? Use of a single driver, especially volume-related, is not proper.

Examination of the data in Table 4.2 suggests that a significant portion of overhead costs is not driven or caused by volume. For example, setup costs are probably related to the number of setups and quality control costs to the number of hours of inspection. Notice that Nitro-Y only has 1.5 times as many setups as the Nitro-X (30/20) and only 1.5 times as many inspection hours (1,200/800). Use of a volume-related cost driver (machine hours or labor hours) and a plantwide rate assigns five times more overhead to the Nitro-Y than to Nitro-X. For quality control and setup costs, then, Nitro-Y is overcosted, and Nitro-X is undercosted.

The problems worsened when departmental rates were used. Nitro-Y consumes 19 times as many direct labor hours (76,000/4,000) as Nitro-X and 5.7 times as many machine hours (34,000/6,000). Thus, Nitro-Y receives 19 times more overhead from department 1 and 5.7 times more overhead from department 2. As Table 4.4 shows, with departmental rates the unit cost of Nitro-X decreases to $8.86, and the unit cost of Nitro-Y increases to $10.87. This change emphasizes the failure of volume-based cost drivers to reflect accurately each product's consumption of setup and quality control costs.

Why Volume-related Cost Drivers Fail

At least two major factors impair the ability of a volume-related cost driver to assign overhead costs accurately: (1) the proportion of non-volume-related overhead costs to total overhead costs and (2) the degree of product diversity.

Non-volume-related overhead costs. In our example, there are four overhead activities: quality control, setup, maintenance and power. Two, maintenance and power, are volume related. Quality control and setup are less dependent on volume. As a result, volume-based cost drivers cannot assign these costs accurately to products.

Using volume-based cost drivers to assign non-volume-related overhead costs creates distorted product costs. The severity of this distortion depends on what proportion of total overhead costs these nonvolume-related costs represent. For our example, setup costs and quality control costs represent a substantial share—51 percent—of total overhead ($170,000/$332,000). This suggests that some care should be exercised in assigning these costs. If non-volume-related overhead costs are only a small percentage of total overhead costs, the distortion of product costs would be quite small. In such a case, the use of volume-based cost drivers may be acceptable.

Product Diversity. When products consume overhead activities in different proportions, a firm has product diversity. To illustrate, the proportion of all overhead activities consumed by both Nitro-X and Nitro-Y is computed and displayed in Table 4.5. The proportion of each activity consumed by a product is defined as the consumption ratio. As you can see from the table, the consumption ratios for these two products differ from the nonvolume-related categories to the volume-related costs.

Table 4.5: Product Diversity: Proportion of Consumption

Overhead Activity	Nitro-X	Nitro-Y	Consumption Measure
Setup	.40(1)	.60(1)	Production runs
Quality control	.40(2)	.60(2)	Inspection hours
Power	.17(3)	.83(3)	Kilowatt hours
Maintenance	.17(4)	.83(4)	Machine hours

(1) 20/50 (Nitro-X) and 30/50 (Nitro-Y)

(2) 800/2,000 (Nitro-X) and 1,200/2,000 (Nitro-Y)

(3) 5,000/30,000 (Nitro-X) and 25,000/30,000 (Nitro-Y)

(4) 10,000/60,000 (Nitro-X) and 50,000/60,000 (Nitro-Y)

Since the non-volume-related overhead costs are a significant proportion of total overhead and their consumption ratio differs from that of the volume-based cost driver, product costs can be distorted if a volume-based cost driver is used. The solution to this costing problem is to use an activity-based costing approach.

Activity-based Product Costing

An activity-based cost system is one which first traces costs to activities and then to products. Traditional product costing also involves two stages, but in the first stage costs are traced to departments, not to activities. In both traditional and activity-based costing, the second stage consists of tracing costs to the product.

The principal difference between the two methods is the number of cost drivers used. Activity-based costing uses a much larger number of cost drivers than the one or two volume-based cost drivers typical in a conventional system. In fact, the approach separates overhead costs into overhead cost pools, where each cost pool is associated with a different cost driver. Then a predetermined overhead rate is computed for each cost pool and each cost driver. In consequence, this method has enhanced accuracy.

Activity-based costing (ABC) is not an alternative costing system to job costing or process costing. It focuses on activities as the principal cost objects. ABC is a method of assigning costs to goods and services and assumes all costs are caused by the activities used to produce those goods and services. This method provides more insight into the causes of costs than conventional costing methods. Conventional costing methods divide the total costs by the number of units to compute a unit cost. In contrast, activity-based costing starts with the detailed activities required to produce a product or service and computes a product's cost using the following four steps:

- Identify the activities that consume resources, and assign costs to those activities. Inspection would be an activity, for example.
- Identify the cost driver(s) associated with each activity or group of activities, known as a cost pool. A cost driver is a factor that causes, or drives, an activity's costs. The number of inspections would be a cost driver. So could the number of times a new drawing is needed because a product has been redesigned.
- Calculate an applied rate for each activity pool. The pool rate could be the cost per purchase order.
- Assign costs to products by multiplying the cost pool rate by the number of cost driver units consumed by the product. For example, the cost per inspection times the number of inspections required for product X for the month of March would measure the cost of inspection activity for product X for March.

Note: ABC is also applicable to service, merchandising, and nonprofit sectors as well as manufacturing companies.

First-stage Procedure

In the first stage of activity-based costing, overhead costs are divided into homogeneous cost pools. A homogeneous cost pool is a collection of overhead costs for which cost variations can be explained by a single cost driver. Overhead activities are homogeneous whenever they have the same consumption ratios for all products. Once a cost pool is defined, the cost per unit of the cost driver is computed for that pool. This is referred to as the pool rate. Computation of the pool rate completes the first stage. Thus, the first stage produces two outcomes: a set of homogeneous cost pools and a pool rate.

For example, in Table 4.5, quality control costs and setup costs can be combined into one homogeneous cost pool and maintenance and power costs into a second. For the first cost pool, the number of production runs or inspection hours could be the cost driver. Since the two cost drivers are perfectly correlated, they will assign the same amount of overhead to both products. For the second pool, machine hours or kilowatt hours could be selected as the cost driver.

Assume for the purpose of illustration that the number of production runs and machine hours are the cost drivers chosen. Using data from Table 4.2, the first-stage outcomes are illustrated in Table 4.6.

Table 4.6: Activity-based Costing: First-stage Procedure

Pool 1:	
Setup costs	$96,000
Quality control costs	74,000
Total costs	$170,000
Production runs	50
Pool rate (Cost per run) $170,000/50	$3,400
Pool 2:	
Power cost	$84,000
Maintenance	78,000
Total costs	$162,000
Machine hours	60,000
Pool rate (Cost per machine hour) $162,000/60,000	$2.70

Second-Stage Procedure

In the second stage, the costs of each overhead pool are traced to products. This is done using the pool rate computed in the first stage and the measure of the amount of resources consumed by each product. This measure is simply the quantity of the cost driver used by each product. In our example, that would be the number of production runs and machine hours used by each product. Thus, the overhead assigned from each cost pool to each product is computed as follows:

Applied overhead = Pool rate x Cost driver units used

To illustrate, consider the assignment of costs from the first overhead pool to Nitro-X. From Table 4.6, the rate for this pool is $3,400 per production run. From Table 4.2, Nitro-X uses 20 production runs. Thus, the overhead assigned from the first cost pool is $68,000 ($3,400 X 20 runs). Similar assignments would be made for the other cost pool and for the other product (for both cost pools).

The total overhead cost per unit of product is obtained by first tracing the overhead costs from the pools to the individual products. This total is then divided by the number of units produced. The result is the unit overhead cost. Adding the per-unit overhead cost to the per-unit prime cost yields the manufacturing cost per unit. In Table 4.7, the manufacturing cost per unit is computed using activity-based costing.

Comparison of Product Costs

In Table 4.8, the unit cost from activity-based costing is compared with the unit costs produced by conventional costing using either a plantwide or departmental rate. This comparison clearly illustrates the effects of using only volume-based cost drivers to assign overhead costs. The activity-based cost reflects the correct pattern of overhead consumption and is, therefore, the most accurate of the three costs shown in Table 4.8. Activity-based product costing reveals that the conventional method undercosts the Nitro-X significantly—by at least 37.7 percent ($14.50 - 10.53)/$10.53 and costs more than the Nitro-Y by at least 8.1 percent ($10.53 - $9.74)/$9.74.

Using only volume-based cost drivers can lead to one product subsidizing another. This subsidy could create the appearance that one group of products is highly profitable and adversely impact the pricing and competitiveness of another group of products. In a highly competitive environment, accurate cost information is critical for sound planning and decision making.

Table 4.7: Activity-based Costing: Second-stage Procedure

Unit Costs	
Nitro-X	
Prime costs	$50,000
Overhead:	
Pool 1: $3,400 X 20	$68,000
Pool 2: $2.70 X 10,000	27,000
Total overhead costs	$95,000
Total manufacturing costs	$145,000
Units produced	10,000
Unit cost	$14.50
Nitro-Y	
Prime costs	$250,000
Overhead:	
Pool 1: $3,400 X 30	$102,000
Pool 2: $2.70 X 50,000	135,000
Total overhead costs	$237,000
Total manufacturing costs	$487,000
Units produced	50,000
Unit cost	$9.74

The Choice of Cost Drivers

At least two major factors should be considered in selecting cost drivers: the cost of measurement and the degree of correlation between the cost driver and the actual consumption of overhead.

The Cost of Measurement. In an activity-based cost system, a large number of cost drivers can be selected and used. However, it is preferable to select cost drivers that use information that is readily available. Information that is not available in the existing system must be produced, which will increase the cost of the firm's information system. A homogeneous cost pool could offer a number of possible cost drivers. For this situation, any cost driver that can be used with existing information should be chosen. This choice minimizes the costs of measurement.

In our example, for instance, quality control costs and setup costs were placed in the same cost pool, giving the choice of using either inspection hours or number of production runs as the cost driver. If the quantities of both cost drivers used by the two products are already being produced by the company's information system, then which is chosen is unimportant. Assume, however, that inspection hours by product are not tracked, but data for production runs are available. In this case, production runs should be chosen as the cost driver, avoiding the need to produce any additional information.

Table 4.8: Comparison of Unit Costs

	Nitro-X	Nitro-Y	Source
Traditional:			
Plantwide rate	10.53	10.53	Table 3
Department rates	8.86	10.87	Table 4
Activity-based costing	$14.50	$9.74	Table 7

Indirect Measures and the Degree of Correlation. The existing information structure can be exploited in another way to minimize the costs of obtaining cost driver quantities. It is sometimes possible to replace a cost driver that directly measures the consumption of an activity with a cost driver that indirectly measures that consumption. For example, inspection hours could be replaced by the actual number of inspections associated with each product; this number is more likely to be known. This replacement only works, of course, if hours used per inspection are reasonably stable for each product. Regression analysis, which will be covered in Chapter 6, can be utilized to determine the degree of correlation. A list of potential cost drivers is given in Table 4.9.

Cost drivers that indirectly measure the consumption of an activity usually measure the number of transactions associated with that activity. It is possible to replace a cost driver that directly measures consumption with one that only indirectly measures it without loss of accuracy provided that the quantities of activity consumed per transaction are stable for each product. In such a case, the indirect cost driver has a high correlation and can be used.

Table 4.9: Cost Drivers

MANUFACTURING:	
Machine hour	Miles driven
Direct labor hour or dollars	Computer time
Number of setups	Square footage
Weight of materials handled	Number of vendors
Number of units reworked	Asset value
Number of orders placed	Number of labor transactions
Number of orders received	Number of units scrapped
Number of inspections	Number of parts
Number of material handling operations	Replacement cost
Number of orders shipped	Design time
Hours of testing time	
NON-MANUFACTURING:	
Number of hospital beds occupied	
Number of surgeries	
Number of take-offs and landings for an airline	
Flight hours	
Number of rooms occupied in a hotel	

The fundamental differences in the traditional and ABC cost systems are summarized in Table 4.10.

Table 4.10: Cost System Comparison

	Traditional	ABC
Cost pools:	One or a limited number	Many to reflect different activities
Applied rate:	Volume-based, Financial	Activity-based, Nonfinancial
Suited for:	Labor-intensive, Low-overhead companies	Capital-intensive, Product-diverse, High-overhead companies
Benefits:	Simple, Inexpensive	Accurate product costing, Possible elimination of nonvalue-added activities

Example 2

Global Metals, Inc. has established the following overhead cost pools and cost drivers for their product:

Overhead Cost Pool	Budgeted Overhead Cost	Cost Driver	Predicted Level for Cost Driver	Predetermined Overhead Rate
Machine set-ups	$100,000	Number of set-ups	100	$1,000 per set-up
Material handling	100,000	Weight of raw material	50,000 pounds	$2.00 per pound
Waste control	50,000	Weight of hazardous chemical used	10,000 pounds	$5.00 per pound
Inspection	75,000	Number of inspections	1,000	$75 per inspection
Other overhead costs	$200,000	Machine Hours	20,000	$10 per machine hour
	$525,000			

Job No. 107 consists of 2,000 special purpose machine tools with the following requirements:

Machine set-ups	2 set-ups
Raw material required	10,000 pounds

Waste material required	2,000 pounds
Inspections	10 inspections
Machine hours	500 machine hours

The overhead assigned to job No. 107 is computed below:

Overhead Cost Pool	Predetermined Overhead Rate	Level of Cost Driver	Assigned Overhead Cost
Machine set-ups	$1,000 per set-up	2 set-ups	$2,000
Material handling	$2.00 per pound	10,000 pounds	20,000
Waste control	$5.00 per pound	2,000 pounds	10,000
Inspection	$75 per inspection	10 inspections	750
Other overhead cost	$10 per machine hour	500 machine hour	5,000
Total			$37,750

The total overhead cost assigned to Job No. 107 is $37,750, or $18.88 per tool ($37,750/2,000). Compare this with the overhead cost that is assigned to the job if the firm uses a single predetermined overhead rate based on machine hours:

Total budgeted overhead cost / Total predicted machine hours

= $525,000 / 20,000

= $26.25 per machine hour

Under this approach, the total overhead cost assigned to job No. 107 is $13,125 ($26.25 per machine hour x 500 machine hours). This is only $6.56 per tool ($13,125/2,000), which is about 1/3 of the overhead cost per tool computed when multiple cost drivers are used.

To summarize:

	ABC	Traditional
Total factory overhead assigned	$37,750	$13,125
Per tool	$18.88	$6.56

The reason for this wide discrepancy is that these special purpose tools require a relatively large number of machine set-ups, a sizable amount of waste materials and several inspections. Thus, they are relatively costly in terms of driving overhead costs. Use of a single predetermined overhead rate obscures that fact.

Inaccurately calculating the overhead cost per unit to the extent illustrated above can have serious adverse consequences for the firm. For example, it can lead to poor decisions about pricing, product mix or contract bidding.

Note: The cost accountant needs to weigh carefully such considerations in designing a product costing system. A costing system using multiple cost drivers is more costly to implement and use, but it may save millions through improved decisions. An ABC approach is expensive to implement and keep. Companies considering ABC should perform a cost-benefit test. The benefits are most significant when a company has

(1) Different products or services that make different demands on resources and

(2) stiff competition where knowledge of costs and cost control is critical.

ABC forces management to think in terms of simplifying operations (activities). Once activities that are consumed by a product are identified, the process can be evaluated with a view to cut costs.

Using Activity-based Costing To Make Marketing Decisions

Marketing cost analysis provides relevant data for managerial decisions to add or drop territories and products. Applying principles of activity-based costing to marketing activities helps marketing managers make decisions about product line or territory profitability. For example, suppose the Nike shoe company considers opening a territory in Russia. The first step is to determine what activities would be required to market shoes in Russia. These activities would include selling, warehousing, order filling, providing credit and collecting on accounts receivable and shipping, in addition to advertising and promotion. The second step is to identify measures of the activities. Some examples of activity measures are shown in Table 4.11. The next step is to estimate the cost of each activity. Finally, management would estimate the number of activities required to open the sales territory in Russia which, multiplied by the cost per activity, would provide an estimate of the cost of marketing in the new territory.

Table 4.11: Activity Cost Drivers

Activity	Measures
Selling	Number of sales calls
	Number of orders obtained
	Volume of sales
Warehousing	Number of items stored
	Volume of items stored
Credit and collection	Number of customer orders
	Dollar amount of customer orders on account

Source: Ronald Lewis, "Activity-Based Costing for Marketing," Management Accounting, November 1991, pp. 33-38.

Activity-based Management

Activity-based management (ABM) is one of the most important ways to be competitive. It is a system wide, integrated approach that focuses management's attention on activities with the goal of improving customer value, reducing costs and working toward the resulting profit. The basic premise of ABM is: Products consume activities; activities consume resources. To be competitive, you must know both the activities that go into manufacturing the products or providing the services and the cost of those activities. To cut down a product's costs, you will likely have to change the activities the product consumes. An attitude such as: I want across-the-board-cuts—everyone reduce cost by 10 percent, rarely obtains the desired results.

In order to achieve desired cost reductions, you must first identify the activities that a product or service consumes. Then you must figure out how to rework those activities to improve productivity and efficiency. Process value analysis is used to try to determine why activities are performed and how well they are performed. Activity-based costing, discussed in this chapter, is also a tool used in activity-based management.

Process Value Analysis

Process value analysis is the method of identifying, describing and evaluating the activities a company performs. It produces the following four outcomes:

1. What activities are done?
2. How many people perform the activities?
3. The time and resources are required to perform the activities.
4. The need to asses the value of the activities to the company, including a recommendation to select and keep only those that add value.

Understanding What Causes Costs

Effective cost control requires managers to understand how producing a product requires activities and how activities, in turn, generate costs. Consider the activities of a manufacturer facing a financial crisis. In a system of managing by the members, each department is told to reduce costs in an amount equal to its share of a proposed budget cut. The usual response by department heads is to reduce the number of people and supplies, as these are the only cost items that they can control in the short run. Asking everyone to work harder produces only temporary gains, however, as the pace cannot be sustained in the long run.

Under ABM, the manufacturer reduces costs by studying what activities it conducts and then develops plans to eliminate nonvalue-added activities and to improve the efficiency of value-added activities. Eliminating activities that do not create customer value is a very effective way to cut costs. For example, spending $100 to train all employees to avoid common mistakes will repay itself many times over by reducing customer ill will caused by those mistakes.

Value-added and Nonvalue-added Activities

A value-added activity is an anything that increases the product's service to the customer. For instance, purchasing the raw materials to make a product is a value-added activity. Without raw materials, the organization would be unable to make the product. Sanding and varnishing a wooden chair are value-added activities because customers do not want poorly-made chairs. Value-added activities are evaluated by how they contribute to the final product's service, quality and cost.

Good management involves finding and, if possible, eliminating nonvalue-added activities. These are activities that when eliminated reduce costs without reducing the product's potential to the customer. In many organizations poor facility layout may require the work in process to be moved around or temporarily stored during production. For example, a Midwest steel company that we studied had more than 100 miles of railroad track to move goods back and forth in a poorly designed facility. Moving work for its own sake around a factory, an office or a store is unlikely to add value for the customer. Waiting, inspecting and storing are other examples of nonvalue-added activities.

Organizations must change the process that makes nonvalue-added activities necessary. Elimination of nonvalue-added activities requires organizations to improve the process so that the activities are no longer required. Organizations strive to reduce or eliminate nonvalue-added activities because, by doing so, they permanently reduce the costs they must incur to produce goods or services without affecting the value to the customer.

Although managers should pay particular attention to nonvalue-added activities, they should also carefully evaluate the need for value-added activities. For example, in wine production, classifying storage as a value-added activity assumes the only way to make good-tasting wine is to allow it to age in storage. Think of the advantage that someone could have if he discovered a way to produce wine that tastes as good as conventionally aged wine but does not require long storage periods.

Activity Drivers and Categories

Activity output is measured by activity drivers. An activity driver is a factor (activity) that causes (drives) costs. We can simply identify activity output measures by classifying activities into four general categories: unit level, batch level product level and facility level. Classifying activities into these general categories is useful because the costs of activities associated with the different levels respond to different types of activity drivers. Table 4.12 describes what they perform, output measures and examples of possible cost drivers.

Table 4.12: Activity Categories and Drivers

	Unit-Level Activities	Batch-Level Activities	Product-Level (Product and Customer-Sustaining) Activities	Facility-Level (Capacity-Sustaining) Activities
Types of activities	Performed each time a unit is produced	Performed each time a batch is produced	Performed as needed to support a product	Sustain a factory's general manufacturing process
Examples:	Direct materials, direct labor, assembly, energy to run machines	Quality inspections, machine setups, production scheduling, material handling	Engineering changes, maintenance of equipment, customer records and files, marketing the product	Plant management, plant security, landscaping, maintaining grounds, heating and lighting, property taxes, rent, plant depreciation
Output measures:	Unit-level drivers	Batch-level drivers	Product-level drivers	Difficult to define
Examples:	Units of product, direct labor hours, machine hours	Number of batches, number of production orders, inspection hours	Number of products, number of changing orders	Plant size (square feet), number of security personnel

The Value Chain Concept of the Business Functions

The value chain concept of the business functions is used throughout the book to demonstrate how to use cost/managerial accounting to add value to organizations

(See Figure 4.1). The value chain describes the linked set of activities that increase time usefulness (or value) of the products and services of an organization (value-added activities). Activities are evaluated by how they contribute to the final product's service, quality and cost. In general, the business functions include the following:

- Research and development—the generation and development of ideas related to new products, services or processes;
- design—the detailed planning and engineering of products, services or processes;
- production—the aggregation and assembly of resources to produce a product or deliver a service;
- marketing—the process that (a) informs potential customers about the attributes of products or services and (b) leads to the purchase of' those products or services;
- distribution—the mechanism established to deliver products or services to customers; and
- customer service—the product or service support activities provided to customers.

A strategy and administration function spans all the business activities described. Human resource management, tax planning, legal matters and the like, for example, potentially affect every step of the value chain. Cost and managerial accounting is a major means of helping managers to run each of the business functions and to coordinate their activities within the framework of the entire organization.

Strategic Cost Analysis

Companies can identify strategic advantages in the marketplace by analyzing the value chain and the information about the costs of activities. A company that eliminates nonvalue-added activities reduces costs without reducing the value of the product to customers. With reduced costs, the company can reduce the price it charges customers, thus giving the company a cost advantage over its competitors. Or the company can use the resources saved from eliminating nonvalue-added activities to provide greater service to customers. Strategic cost analysis is the use of cost data to develop and identify superior strategies that will produce a sustainable competitive advantage. The idea here is simple. Look for activities that are not on the value chain. If' the company can safely eliminate nonvalue-added activities, then it should do so. By identifying and cutting them, you will save the company money and make it more competitive.

Figure 4.1: The Value Chain and Cost/Management Accounting

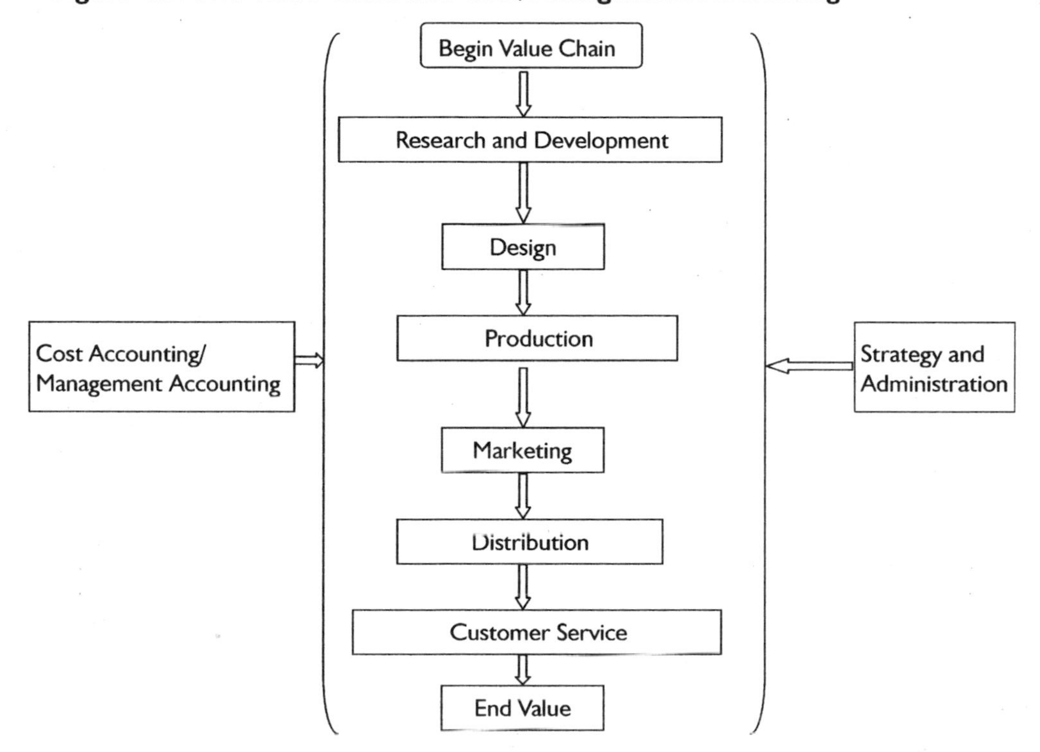

Another approach to gaining a cost advantage is to identify where on the value chain your company has a strategic advantage. Many computer software companies, for example, are looking at foreign markets as a way to capitalize on their investment in research and development. The reservoir of intellectual capital gives these firms an advantage over local competitors who have not yet developed this expertise. These competitors would face research and development costs already incurred by established companies, making it difficult for the newcomers to charge competitive prices and still make a profit.

Chapter Summary

The chapter discussed in detail how activity costing provides more accurate product cost figures for product costing and pricing, using multiple overhead cost pools and cost drivers. Conventional cost systems are not able to assign the costs of nonvolume-related overhead activities accurately. For this reason, assigning overhead using only volume-based drivers or a single driver can distort product costs.

Two examples were provided to illustrate the use of the ABC system versus the traditional system using a single driver such as machine hours or direct labor hours.

Activity-based costing may provide more accurate information about product costs. It helps managers make better decisions about product design, pricing, marketing, and mix, and encourages continual operating improvements. Activity-based management (ABM), of which ABC is a tool, was discussed.

Chapter 5

Break-even and Cost-volume-profit Analysis

Cost-volume-profit (CVP) analysis, together with cost behavior information, helps managerial accountants perform many useful analyses. CVP analysis deals with how profit and costs change with a change in volume. More specifically, it looks at the effects on profits of changes in such factors as variable costs, fixed costs, selling prices, volume and mix of products sold. By studying the relationships of costs, sales and net income, management is better able to cope with many planning decisions.

Break-even analysis, a branch of CVP analysis, determines the break-even in sales. Break-even point—the financial crossover point when revenues exactly match costs—does not show up in corporate earnings reports, but managerial accountants find it an extremely useful measurement in a variety of ways.

Questions Answered by CVP Analysis

CVP analysis tries to answer the following questions:

(a) What sales volume is required to break even?

(b) What sales volume is necessary to earn a desired profit?

(c) What profit can be expected on a given sales volume?

(d) How would changes in selling price, variable costs, fixed costs and output affect profits?

(e) How would a change in the mix of products sold affect the break-even and target income volume and profit potential?

Contribution Margin (CM)

For accurate CVP analysis, a distinction must be made between costs as being either variable or fixed. Mixed costs must be separated into their variable and fixed components. In order to compute the break-even point and perform various CVP analyses, note the following important concepts.

Contribution margin (CM). The contribution margin is the excess of sales (S) over the variable costs (VC) of the product or service. It is the amount of money available to cover fixed costs (FC) and to generate profit. Symbolically:

$$CM = S - VC.$$

Unit contribution margin. The unit CM is the excess of the unit selling price (p) less the unit variable cost (v). Symbolically:

$$\text{Unit CM} = p - v.$$

Contribution margin ratio. The CM ratio is the contribution margin as a percentage of sales, i.e.:

$$\text{CM Ratio} = \frac{CM}{S} = \frac{(S-VC)}{S} = 1 - \frac{VC}{S}$$

The CM ratio can also be computed using per-unit data as follows:

$$\text{CM Ratio} = \frac{\text{Unit CM}}{p} = \frac{(p-v)}{p} = 1 - \frac{v}{p}$$

Note that the CM ratio is 1 minus the variable cost ratio. For example, if variable costs are 40 percent of sales, then the variable cost ratio is 40 percent and the CM ratio is 60 percent.

Example 1

To illustrate the various concepts of CM, consider the following data for Porter Toy Store:

	Total	Per Unit	Percentage
Sales (1,500 units)	$37,500	$25	100%
Less: Variable costs	15,000	10	40
Contribution margin	$22,500	$15	60%
Less: Fixed costs	15,000		
Net income	$7,500		

From the data listed above, CM, unit CM, and the CM ratio are computed as:

$CM = S - VC = \$37,500 - \$15,000 = \$22,500$

$\text{Unit CM} = p - v = \$25 - \$10 = \$15$

$\text{CM Ratio} = CM / S = \$22,500 / \$37,500 = 1 - (\$15,000 / \$37,500)$

$= 1 - 0.4 = 0.6 = 60\%$

or

$= \text{Unit CM} / p = \$15 / \$25 = 0.6 = 60\%$

Break-even Analysis

The break-even point represents the level of sales revenue that equals the total of the variable and fixed costs for a given volume of output at a particular capacity use rate. For example, you might want to ask the break-even occupancy rate (or vacancy rate) for a hotel or the break-even load rate for an airliner.

Generally, the lower the break-even point, the higher the profit and the less the operating risk, other things being equal. The break-even point also provides managerial accountants with insights into profit planning. It can be computed in three different ways: the equation approach, contribution approach and graphical approach. The equation approach is based on the cost-volume-profit equation which shows the relationships among sales, variable and fixed costs, and net income.

$S = VC + FC + \text{Net Income}$

At the break-even volume, $S = VC + FC + 0$. Defining x = volume in units, the above relationship can be written in terms of x:

$px = vx + FC$

$(p-v)x = FC$

Solving for x yields the following formula for break-even sales volume:

$$x = \frac{FC}{(p-v)} = \frac{\text{Fixed Costs}}{\text{Unit CM}}$$

$$\text{Break-even point in dollars (S)} = \frac{\text{Fixed Costs}}{\text{CM Ratio}}$$

Note: The sales revenue needed to breakeven is that point at which the company covers all costs but generates no income.

$S = VC + FC + 0$

$S = (VC/S)S + FC$

$(1 - VC/S)S = FC$

$$S = \frac{FC}{(1 - VC/S)} = \frac{\text{Fixed Costs}}{(1 - \text{Variable Cost Ratio})} = \frac{\text{Fixed Costs}}{\text{CM Ratio}}$$

Example 2

Using the same data given in Example 1, where unit CM = $25 - $10 = $15 and CM ratio = 60%, we get:

Break-even point in units = $15,000/$15 = 1,000 units

Break-even point in dollars = 1,000 units X $25 = $25,000

Or, alternatively, $15,000/0.6 = $25,000

Graphical Approach in a Spreadsheet Format

The graphical approach to obtaining the break-even point is based on the so-called break-even (B-E) chart as shown in Figure 5.1. Sales revenue, variable costs and fixed costs are plotted on the vertical axis while volume is plotted on the horizontal axis. The break-even point is the point where the total sales revenue line intersects the total cost line. The chart can also effectively report profit potentials over a wide range of activity and therefore be used as a tool for discussion and presentation.

The profit-volume (P-V) chart as shown in Figure 5.2, focuses directly on how profits vary with changes in volume. Profits are plotted on the vertical axis while units of output are shown on the horizontal axis. The P-V chart provides a quick condensed comparison of how alternatives on pricing, variable costs, or fixed costs may affect net income as volume changes. The P-V chart can be easily constructed from the B-E chart. Note that the slope of the chart is the unit CM.

Determination of Target Income Volume

Besides determining the break-even point, CVP analysis determines the sales required to attain a particular income level or target net income. There are two ways in which target net income can be expressed:

Case 1. As a specific dollar amount

Case 2. As a percentage of sales

Case 1

As a specific dollar amount, the formula is:

$$\text{Target income sales volume} = \frac{\text{Fixed Costs + Target Income}}{\text{Unit CM}}$$

Case 2

Specifying target income as a percentage of sales, the cost-volume equation is

$$px = vx + FC + \%(px)$$

Solving this for x yields:

$$\frac{FC}{p - v - \%(p)}$$

In words:

$$\text{Target income sales volume} = \frac{\text{Fixed Costs}}{\text{Unit CM} - (\text{\% of Unit Price Sales})}$$

Example 3

Using the same data given in Example 1, assume that Porter Toy Store wishes to attain:

Case 1. A target income of $15,000 before tax

Case 2. A target income of 20% of sales

In Case 1, the target income volume would be:

($15,000 + $15,000) / ($25 - $10) = $30,000 / $15 = 2,000 Units

In Case 2, the target income volume required is:

$15,000/[($25 - $10 – (20%)($25)] = $15,000/($15 - $5) = 1,500 Units

Impact of Income Taxes

If target income (expressed as a specific dollar amount) is given on an after-tax basis, an adjustment is necessary before we use the previous formula. The reason is that the profit target is expressed in before-tax terms. Therefore, the after-tax target income must be first converted to a before-tax target, as follows:

$$\text{Before-tax target income} = \frac{\text{After-tax Target Income}}{(1 - \text{Tax Rate})}$$

Example 1

Assume in Example 1 that Porter Toy Store wants to achieve an after-tax income of $6,000. The tax rate is 40 percent. Then, the first step is:

$$\frac{\$6,000}{(1 - 0.4)} = \$10,000$$

The second step is to plug this figure into our regular formula as follows:

Target income volume = (\$15,000 + \$10,000) / 15 = 1,667 Units

Margin of Safety

The margin of safety is a measure of difference between the actual sales and the break-even sales. It is the amount by which sales revenue may drop before losses begin, and is expressed as a percentage of expected sales:

$$\text{Margin of Safety} = \frac{(\text{Expected Sales} - \text{Breakeven Sales})}{\text{Expected Sales}}$$

The margin of safety is used as a measure of operating risk. The larger the ratio, the safer the situation since there is less risk of reaching the break-even point.

Example 5

Assume Porter Toy Store projects sales of \$35,000 with a break-even sales level of \$25,000. The projected margin of safety is:

(\$35,000 - \$25,000) / \$35,000 = 28.57%

Figure 5.1: Breakeven Chart

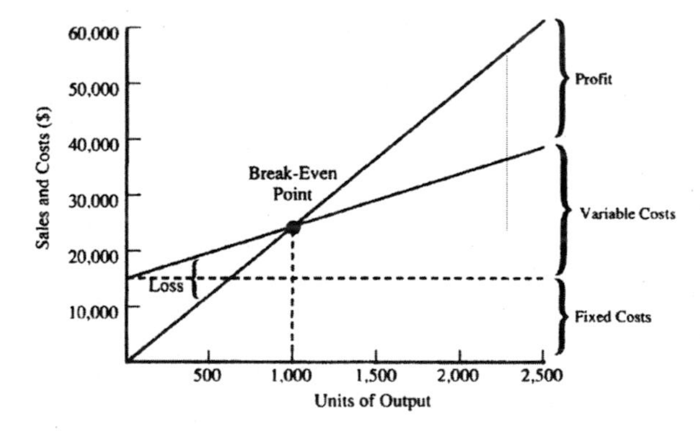

Figure 5.2: Profit-volume (P–V) Chart

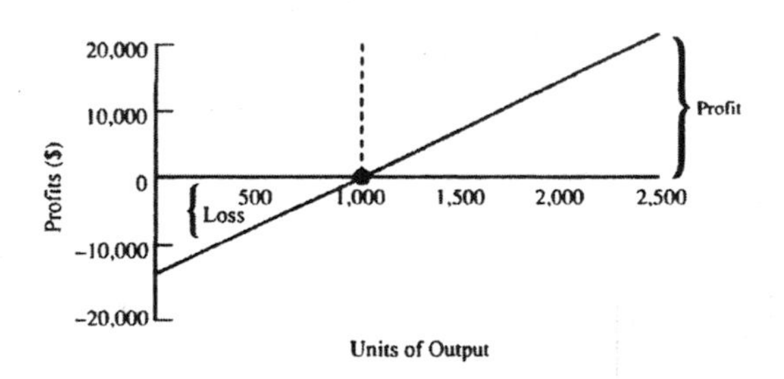

Some Applications of CVP Analysis and What-if Analysis

The concepts of contribution margin and the contribution income statement have many applications in profit planning and short-term decision making. Many what-if scenarios can be evaluated using them as planning tools, especially utilizing a spreadsheet program such as Excel. Some applications are illustrated in Examples 6 to 10 using the same data as in Example 1.

Example 6

Recall from Example 1 that Porter Toy Store has a CM of 60 percent and fixed costs of $15,000 per period. Assume that the store expects sales to go up by $10,000 for the next period. How much will income increase?

Using the CM concepts, we can quickly compute the impact of a change in sales on profits. The formula for computing the impact is:

Change in net income = Dollar change in sales x CM ratio

Thus:

Increase in net income = $10,000 X 60% = $6,000

Therefore, the income will go up by $6,000, assuming there is no change in fixed costs.

If we are given a change in unit sales instead of dollars, then the formula becomes:

Change in net income = Change in unit sales x Unit CM

Example 7

Assume that the store expects sales to go up by 400 units. How much will income increase? From Example 1, the store's unit CM is $15.Again, assuming there is no change in fixed costs, the income will increase by $6,000.

400 units x $15 = $6,000

Example 8

What net income is expected on sales of $47,500? The answer is the difference between the CM and the fixed costs:

CM: $47,500 X 60%	$28,500
Less: Fixed costs	15,000
Net income	$13,500

Example 9

Porter Toy Store is considering increasing the advertising budget by $5,000, which would increase sales revenue by $8,000. Should the advertising budget be increased?

The answer is no, since the increase in the CM is less than the increased cost:

Increase in CM: $8,000 X 60%	$4,800
Increase in advertising	5,000
Decrease in net income	$(200)

Example 10

Consider the original data. Assume again that Porter Toy Store is currently selling 1,500 units per period. In an effort to increase sales, management is considering cutting its unit price by $5 and increasing the advertising budget by $1,000. If these two steps are taken, management feels that unit sales will go up by 60 percent. Should the two steps be taken?

A $5 reduction in the selling price will cause the unit CM to decrease from $15 to $10. Thus:

Proposed CM: 2,400 units X $10	$24,000
Present CM: 1,500 units X $15	22,500
Increase in CM	$1,500
Increase in advertising outlay	1,000
Increase in net income	$500

The answer, therefore, is yes. Alternatively, the same answer can be obtained by developing comparative income statements in a contribution format:

	(A) Present (1,500 units)	(B) Proposed (2,400 units)	(B - A) Difference
Sales	$37,500 (@$25)	$48,000 (@$20)	$10,500
Less: Variable cost	15,000 (@$10)	24,000 (@$10)	9,000
CM	$22,500	$24,000	$1,500
Less: Fixed costs	15,000	16,000	1,000
Net income	$ 7,500	$ 8,000	$500

Sales Mix Analysis

Break-even and cost-volume-profit analysis requires some additional computations and assumptions when a company produces and sells more than one product. In multi-product firms, sales mix is an important factor in calculating an overall company break-even point.

As a result, the break-even points and cost-volume-profit relationships vary with the relative proportions of the products sold, called the sales mix.

Different selling prices and different variable costs result in different unit CM and CM ratios. In break-even and CVP analysis, it is necessary to predetermine the sales mix and then compute a weighted average unit CM. It is also necessary to assume that the sales mix does not change for a specified period. The break-even formula for the company as a whole is:

$$\text{Break-even sales in units (or in dollars)} = \frac{\text{Fixed Costs}}{\text{Weighted Average Unit CM (or CM Ratio)}}$$

Example 11

Assume that Knibex, Inc. produces cutlery sets out of high-quality wood and steel. The company makes a deluxe cutlery set and a standard set that have the following unit CM data:

	Deluxe	Standard
Selling price	$15	$10
Variable cost per unit	12	5
Unit CM	$3	$5
Sales mix	60%	40%
	(based on sales volume)	
Fixed costs	$76,000	

The weighted average unit CM = ($3)(0.6) + ($5)(0.4) = $3.80. Therefore, the company's break-even point in units is:

$76,000/$3.80 = 20,000 units

which is divided as follows:

Deluxe:	20,000 units x 60% =	12,000 units
Standard:	20,000 units x 40% =	8,000
		20,000 units

Example 12

Assume that Dante, Inc. is a producer of recreational equipment. It expects to produce and sell three types of sleeping bags—the Economy, the Regular and the Backpacker. Information on the bags is given below:

	Economy	Budgeted Regular	Backpacker	Total
Sales	$30,000	$60,000	$10,000	$100,000
Sales mix	30%	60%	10%	100%
Less VC	24,000	40,000	5,000	69,000
	(80%)	(66 2/3%)	(50%)	
CM	$6,000	$20,000	$5,000	$31,000
CM ratio	20%	33 1/3%	50%	31%
Fixed costs				$18,600
Net income				$12,400

The CM ratio for Dante, Inc. is $31,000/$100,000 = 31 percent.

Therefore the break-even point in dollars is:

$18,600/0.31 = $60,000

which will be split in the mix ratio of 3:6:1 to give us the following break-even points for the individual products:

Economy:	$60,000 x 30% =	$18,000
Regular:	$60,000 x 60% =	36,000
Backpacker:	$60,000 x 10% =	6,000
		$60,000

One of the most important assumptions underlying CVP analysis in a multi-product firm is that the sales mix will not change during the planning period. But if the sales mix changes, the break-even point will also change.

Example 13

Assume that total sales from Example 12 was achieved at $100,000 but that an actual mix came out differently from the budgeted mix (i.e., for Economy, 30 percent to 55 percent, for Regular, 60 percent to 40 percent, and for Backpacker, 10 percent to 5 percent).

	Economy	Actual Regular	Backpacker	Total
Sales	$55,000	$40,000	$5,000	$100,000
Sales mix	55%	40%	5%	100%
Less: VC	44,000	26,667*	2,500**	73,167
CM	$11,000	$13,333	$2,500	$26,833
CM ratio	20%	33 1/3%	50%	26.83%
Fixed Costs				$18,600
Net income				$8,233

* $26,667 = $40,000 x (100% - 33 1/3%) = $40,000 x 66 2/3%

* $2,500 = $5,000 x (100% - 50%) = $5,000 x 50%

Note: The shift in sales mix toward the less profitable line, Economy, has caused the CM ratio for the company as a whole to drop from 31 percent to 26.83 percent.

The new break-even point will be $18,600/0.2683 = $69,325

The break-even dollar volume has increased from $60,000 to $69,325.

You should remember

The deterioration (improvement) in the mix caused net income to go down (up). It is important to note that generally, the shift of emphasis from low-margin products to high-margin ones will increase the overall profits of the company.

Assumptions Underlying Break-Even and CVP Analysis

The basic break-even and CVP models are subject to a number of limiting assumptions. They are:

(a) The selling price per unit is constant throughout the entire relevant range of activity.

(b) All costs are classified as fixed or variable.

(c) The variable cost per unit is constant.

(d) There is only one product or a constant sales mix.

(e) Inventories do not change significantly from period to period.

(f) Volume is the only factor affecting variable costs.

Chapter Summary

Cost-volume-profit analysis is useful as a frame of reference, as a vehicle for expressing overall managerial performance, and as a planning device via break-even techniques and what-if scenarios. The following points highlight the analytical usefulness of CVP analysis as a tool for profit planning:

1. A change in either the selling price or the variable cost per unit alters CM or the CM ratio and thus the break-even point.
2. As sales exceed the break-even point, a higher unit CM or CM ratio will result in greater profits than a small unit CM or CM ratio.
3. The lower the break-even sales, the less risky the business is and the safer the investment is, other things being equal.
4. A large margin of safety means lower operating risk since a large decrease in sales can occur before losses are experienced
5. Using the contribution income statement model and a spreadsheet program such as Excel, a variety of what-if planning and decision scenarios can be evaluated.

In a multi-product firm, sales mix is often more important than overall market share. The emphasis on high-margin products tends to maximize overall profits of the firm.

Chapter 6

Analysis of Cost Behavior and Cost Estimation

Not all costs behave in the same way. There are certain costs that vary in proportion to changes in volume or activity, such as labor hours and machine hours. There are other costs that do not change even though volume changes. An understanding of cost behavior is helpful:

1. For break-even and cost-volume-profit analysis;
2. to appraise divisional performance;
3. for flexible budgeting;
4. to make short-term choice decisions; and
5. to make transfer decisions.

A Further Look at Costs by Behavior

As was discussed in Chapter 2, depending on how a cost will react or respond to changes in the level of activity, costs may be viewed as variable, fixed or mixed (semi-variable). This classification is made within a specified range of activity, called the relevant range. The relevant range is the volume zone within which the behavior of variable costs, fixed costs and selling prices can be predicted with reasonable accuracy.

Variable costs, also known as engineered costs, vary in total with changes in volume or level of activity. Examples of variable costs include the costs of direct materials, direct labor and sales commissions. The following factory overhead items fall in the variable cost category:

Variable factory overhead:

Supplies	Receiving costs
Fuel and power	Overtime premium
Spoilage and defective work	

Fixed costs do not change in total regardless of the volume or level of activity. Examples include advertising expense, salaries and depreciation. The following factory overhead items fall in the fixed cost category:

Fixed factory overhead:

Property taxes	Rent on factory building
Depreciation	Indirect labor
Insurance	Patent amortization

As previously discussed, mixed costs contain both a fixed element and a variable one. Salespersons' compensation, including salary and commission, is an example. The following factory overhead items may be considered mixed costs:

Mixed Factory Overhead:

Supervision	Maintenance and repairs
Inspection	Workmen's compensation insurance
Service department costs	Employer's payroll taxes
Utilities	Rental of delivery truck
Fringe benefits	Quality costs
Cleanup costs	

Note that factory overhead, taken as a whole, would be a perfect example of mixed costs. Figure 6.1 displays how each of these three types of costs varies with changes in volume.

Types of Fixed Costs – Committed or Discretionary

Strictly speaking, there is no such thing as a fixed cost. In the long run, all costs are variable. In the short run, however, some fixed costs, called discretionary (or managed or programmed) fixed costs, will change. It is important to note that these costs change because of managerial decisions, not because of changes in volume. Examples of discretionary types of fixed costs are advertising, training, research and development.

Another type of fixed costs, called committed (or capacity) fixed costs, are those costs that do not change and are the results of commitments previously made. Fixed costs such as rent, depreciation, insurance and executive salaries are committed fixed costs since management has committed itself for a long period of time regarding the company's production facilities and manpower requirements.

Analysis of Mixed (Semi-variable) Costs

For planning, control, and decision making purposes, mixed costs need to be separated into their variable and fixed components. Since the mixed costs contain both fixed and variable elements, the analysis takes the following mathematical form, which is called a cost-volume formula (flexible budget formula or cost function):

$$y = a + bx$$

where y = the mixed cost to be broken up.

x = any given measure of activity (cost driver) such as direct labor hours, machine hours, or production volume.

a = the fixed cost component. b = the variable rate per unit of x.

Relevant Range

Management quite often uses the notion of relevant range in estimating cost behavior. The relevant range is the range of activity over which the company expects a set of cost behaviors to be consistent (or linear). For example, if the relevant range of activity is between 10,000 and 20,000 units of cars, the auto maker assumes that certain costs are fixed and while others are variable within that range.

Separating the mixed cost into its fixed and variable components is the same thing as estimating the parameter values a and b in the cost-volume formula. There are several methods available to be used for this purpose including the high-low method and the least-squares method (regression analysis). They are discussed below.

Engineering Analysis

Engineering analysis measures cost behavior according to what costs should be, not by what costs have been. It entails a systematic review of materials, labor, support services and facilities needed for product and services. Engineers use time and motion studies and similar engineering methods to estimate what costs should be from engineers' specifications of the inputs required to manufacture a unit of output or to perform a particular service. This can be used for existing products or for new products similar to what has been produced before. Disadvantages of this method are that it is prohibitively costly and often not timely. Further its is difficult to estimate indirect costs. The engineering method is most useful when costs involved are variable costs, where there is a clear input/output relation.

Account Analysis

Account analysis selects a volume-related cost driver, and classifies each account from the accounting records as a variable or fixed cost. The cost accountant then looks at each cost account balance and estimates either the variable cost per unit of cost driver activity or the periodic fixed cost. Account analysis requires a detailed examination of the data, presumably by cost accountants and managers who are familiar with the activities of the company, and the way the company's activities affect costs. Because account analysis is judgmental, different analysts are likely to provide different estimates of cost behavior.

Example 1

The cafeteria department of Los Al Health Center reported the following costs for October 20X1:

Monthly Cost	October 20X1 Amount
Food and beverages	$9,350
Hourly wages and benefits	18,900
Supervisor's salary	4,000
Equipment depreciation and rental	6,105
Supplies	2,760
Total cafeteria costs	$41,115

The cafeteria served 11,520 meals during the month. Using an account analysis to classify costs, we can determine the cost function. Note that in this example, the supervisor's salary ($4,000 per month) and the equipment depreciation and rental ($6,105 per month) are fixed while the remainder ($31,010) varies with the cost driver, i.e., the number of meals served. Dividing the variable costs by the number of meals served yields $2.692 and the department's cost-volume formula is:

$10,105 + $2.692 per meal.

The High-low Method

The high-low method, as the name indicates, uses two extreme data points to determine the values of a (the fixed cost portion) and b (the variable rate) in the equation Y = a + bX. The extreme data points are the highest representative X-Y pair and the lowest representative X-Y pair. The activity level X, rather than the mixed cost item y, governs their selection.

The high-low method is explained, step by step, as follows:

Step 1 Select the highest pair and the lowest pair

Step 2 Compute the variable rate, b, using the formula:

Difference in cost Y

$$\text{Variable rate} = \frac{\text{Difference in cost Y}}{\text{Difference in activity X}}$$

X Difference in activity X

Step 3 Compute the fixed cost portion as:

Fixed cost portion = Total mixed cost - Variable cost (or a = Y – bX)

Example 2

Flexible Manufacturing Company decided to relate total factory overhead costs to direct labor hours (DLH) to develop a cost-volume formula in the form of Y = a + bX. Twelve monthly observations are collected. They are given in Table 6.1 and plotted as shown in Figure 6.2.

Table 6.1

Month	Direct Labor Hours (X) (000 omitted)	Factory Overhead (Y) (000 omitted)
January	9 hours	$15
February	19	20
March	11	14
April	14	16
May	23	25
June	12	20
July	12	20
August	22	23
September	7	14
October	13	22
November	15	18
December	17	18
Total	174 hours	$225

The high-low points selected from the monthly observations are:

	X	Y
High	23 hours	$25 (May pair)
Low	7	$14 (September pair)
Difference	16 hours	$11

Figure 6.2: Scatter Diagram

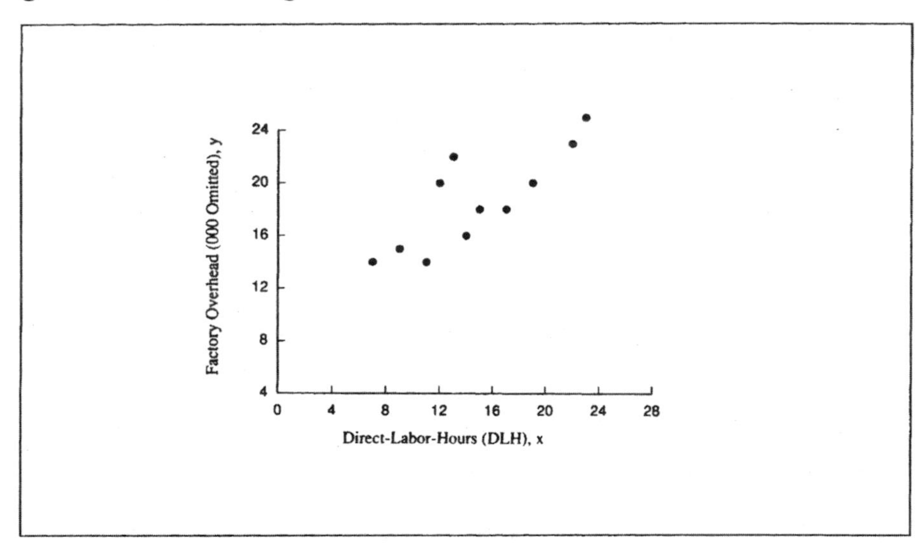

Thus:

$$\text{Variable rate b} = \frac{\text{Difference in Y}}{\text{Difference in X}} = \frac{\$11}{16 \text{ hours}} = \$0.6875 \text{ per DLH}$$

The fixed cost portion is computed as:

	High	Low
Factory overhead (y)	$25	$14
Variable expense($0.6875 per DLH)	(15.8125)*	(4.8125)*
	9.1875	9.1875

*$0.6875 x 23 hours = $15.8125; $0.6875 x 7 hours = $4.8125

Therefore, the cost-volume formula for factory overhead is:

$9.1875 fixed plus $0.6875 per DLH.

The high-low method is simple and easy to use. It has the disadvantage, however, of using two extreme data points, which may not be representative of normal conditions. The method may yield unreliable estimates of a and b in our formula. In such a case, it would be wise to drop them and choose two other points that are more representative of normal situations. Be sure to check the scatter diagram for this possibility.

Note: Regardless of choice of the method, whether the high-low method—or the least-squares method, for that matter—the analyst must plot the observed data on a scatter diagram (also called a scattergraph or scatterplot). The reason is that the relationship between y and x shows a linear pattern in order to justify the use of the linear form $y = a + bx$.

Especially for the high-low method, with a scatter diagram it is easier to locate the highest and lowest pairs on the diagram than on the table and it allows the analyst to ensure that the two points chosen are not extreme (i.e., they must be representative of the normal behavior).

Regression Analysis

One popular method for estimating the cost-volume formula is regression analysis. Regression analysis is a statistical procedure for estimating mathematically the average relationship between the dependent variable and the independent variable(s). Simple regression involves one independent variable, e.g., DLH or machine hours alone, whereas multiple regression involves two or more activity variables.

In this chapter, we will discuss simple (linear) regression to illustrate the least-squares method, which means that we will assume the $Y = a + bX$ relationship. Unlike the high-low method, in an effort to estimate the variable rate and the fixed cost portion, the regression method includes all the observed data and attempts to find a line of best fit. To find this line, a technique called the least-squares method is used. To explain the least-squares method, we define the error as the difference between the observed value and the estimated one of some mixed cost and denote it with u.

Symbolically, $u = Y - Y'$

where Y = observed value of a semivariable expense

Y' = estimated value based on $Y' = a + bX$

The least-squares criterion requires that the line of best fit be such that the sum of the squares of the errors (or the vertical distance in Figure 6.3 from the observed data points to the line) is a minimum, i.e.:

Minimum: $\sum u^2 = \sum(Y - Y')^2 = \sum(Y-a-bX)^2$

Figure 6.3: Y and Y'

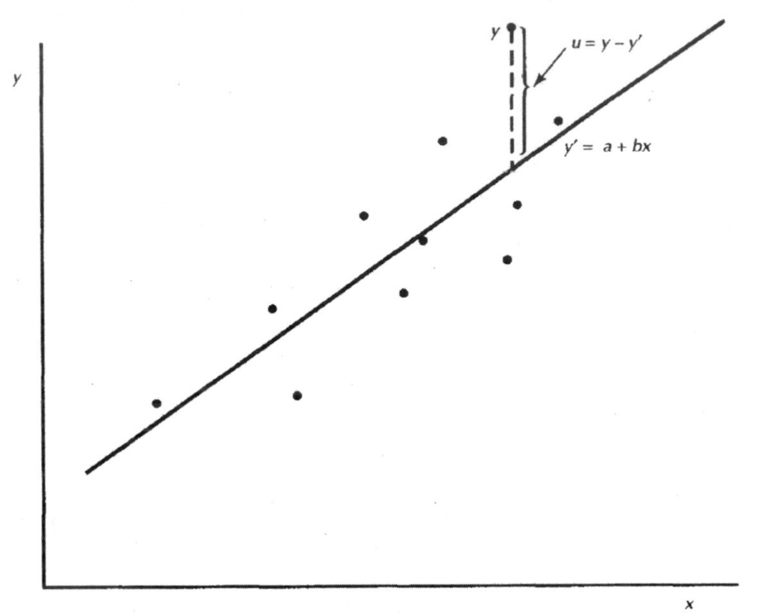

Using differential calculus we obtain the following equations, called normal equations:

$$\sum Y = na + b\sum X$$

$$\sum XY = a\sum X + b\sum X^2$$

Solving the equations for b and a yields:

$$b = \frac{n\sum XY - (\sum X)(\sum Y)}{n\sum X^2 - (\sum X)^2}$$

$$a = \overline{Y} - b\overline{X}$$

$$\text{where } \overline{Y} = \frac{\sum Y}{n} \text{ and } \overline{X} = \frac{\sum X}{n}$$

Example 3

To illustrate the computations of b and a, we will refer to the data in Table 6.2. All the sums required are computed and shown below.

Table 6.2

DLH (X)		Factory Overhead (Y)	XY	X^2	Y^2
	9 hours	$15	135	81	225
19		20	380	361	400
11		14	154	121	196
14		16	224	196	256
23		25	575	529	625
12		20	240	144	400
12		20	240	144	400
22		23	506	484	529
7		14	98	49	196
13		22	286	169	484
15		18	270	225	324
17		18	306	289	324
	174 hours	$225	3,414	2,792	4,359

From the table above:

$\Sigma X = 174$; $\Sigma Y = 225$; $\Sigma XY = 3{,}414$; $\Sigma X^2 = 2{,}792$.

$= \Sigma X/n = 174/12 = 14.5$; $= \Sigma Y/n = 225/12 = 18.75$.

Substituting these values into the formula for b first:

$$b = \frac{n\sum XY - (\sum X)(\sum Y)}{n\sum X^2 - (\sum X)^2} = \frac{(12)(3{,}414)-(174)(225)}{(12)(2{,}792)-(174)^2} = \frac{1{,}818}{3{,}228} = 0.5632$$

$$a = \overline{Y} - b\overline{X} = 18.75 - (0.5632)(14.5) = 18.75 - 8.1664 = 10.5836$$

The cost-volume formula then is:

$Y' = \$10.5836 + \$0.5632\,X$

or $10.5836 fixed, plus $0.5632 per DLH

Note: $\sum Y^2$ is not used here but rather is computed for future use.

Example 4

Assume that the direct labor hours of 10 are to be expended for next year. The projected factory overhead for the next year would be computed as follows:

$$
\begin{aligned}
Y' &= 10.5836 + 0.5632\,X \\
&= 10.5836 + 0.5632\,(10) \\
&= \$16.2156
\end{aligned}
$$

Regression Statistics

Unlike the high-low method, regression analysis is a statistical method. It uses a variety of statistics to tell about the accuracy and reliability of the regression results. They include:

1. correlation coefficient (R) and coefficient of determination (R^2)
2. standard error of the estimate (S_e) and prediction confidence interval
3. standard error of the regression coefficient (S_b) and t-statistic

   (Only the first ones are within the scope of this book.)

Correlation Coefficient (R) and Coefficient of Determination (R^2)

The correlation coefficient R measures the degree of correlation between Y and X. The range of values it takes on is between -1 and +1. More widely used, however, is the coefficient of determination, designated R^2 (read as R-squared).

Simply put, R^2 tells us how good the estimated regression equation is. In other words, it is a measure of "goodness of fit" in the regression. Therefore, the higher the R^2, the more confidence we have in our cost volume formula.

More specifically, the coefficient of determination represents the proportion of the total variation in Y that is explained by the regression equation. It has the range of values between 0 and 1.

You should remember

A low R^2 is an indication that the model is inadequate for explaining the y variable.

The general causes for this problem are:

1. Use of a wrong functional form;
2. poor choice of an X variable as the predictor; and
3. the omission of some important variable or variables from the model.

Note: R^2 is a measure of goodness of fit. Even though the line, obtained by the use of the least-squared error rule, is supposed to be the line of best-fit, it may still be inaccurate. The least-square line may have been the best among the linear lines. The observed data, however, may exhibit a curvilinear pattern, which cannot be visualized especially in multiple regressions. In other words, since it is impossible to draw the scatter diagram in a multi-variable situation, we must rely on a statistic such as R^2 to determine the degree of the goodness of fit. Note that low values of R^2 indicate that the cost driver does not fully explain cost behavior.

Example 5

The statement: Factory overhead is a function of direct labor hours with $R^2 = 70$ percent, can be interpreted as 70 percent of the total variation of factory overhead is explained by the regression equation or the change in direct labor hours and the remaining 30 percent is accounted for by something other than direct labor hours, such as machine hours.

The coefficient of determination is computed as:

$$R^2 = 1 - \frac{\sum(Y - Y')^2}{\sum(Y - \bar{Y})^2}$$

In a simple regression situation, however, there is a short-cut method available:

$$R^2 = \frac{[n\sum XY - (\sum X)(\sum Y)]^2}{[n\sum X^2 - (\sum X)^2][n\sum Y^2 - (\sum Y)^2]}$$

Comparing this formula with the one for b, we see that the only additional information we need to compute R^2 is ΣY^2.

Note: For computational ease, we often calculate r first, using:

$$R = \frac{n\sum XY - (\sum X)(\sum Y)}{\sqrt{[n\sum X^2 - (\sum X)^2]}\sqrt{[n\sum Y^2 - (\sum Y)^2]}}$$

and then square R i.e. $R^2 = (R)^2$

Example 6

To illustrate the computations of various regression statistics, we will refer to the data in Table 6.1. Using the shortcut method for R^2:

$$R^2 = \frac{(1{,}818)^2}{[3{,}228][(12)(4{,}359) - (225)^2]} = \frac{3{,}305{,}124}{[3{,}228][52{,}308 - 50{,}625]} = \frac{3{,}305{,}124}{(3{,}228)(1{,}683)}$$

$$= \frac{3{,}305{,}124}{5{,}432{,}724} = 0.6084 = 60.84\%$$

This means that about 60.84 percent of the total variation in factory overhead is explained by direct labor hours and the remaining 39.16 percent is still unexplained. A relatively low R^2 indicates that there is a lot of room for improvement in our estimated cost volume formula (Y' = \$10.5836 + \$0.5632X). Machine hours or a combination of direct labor hours and machine hours might improve R^2.

Use of a Spreadsheet Program for Regression

We can use a electronic spreadsheet program such as Excel in order to develop a model and estimate most of the statistics we discussed thus far.

To utilize Excel for regression analysis, the following procedure needs to be followed:

1. Click the Tools menu.
2. Click Add-Ins.
3. Click Analysis ToolPak. (If Analysis ToolPak is not listed among your available add-ins, exit Excel, double-click the MS Excel Setup icon, click Add/Remove, double-click Add-Ins, and select Analysis ToolPak. Then restart Excel and repeat the above instruction.)

After ensuring that the Analysis ToolPak is available, you can access the regression tool by completing the following steps:

1. Click the Tools menu.
2. Click Data Analysis.
3. Click Regression

Note: To obtain a scattergraph, use Excel's Chart Wizard.

Figure 6.4 shows the Excel regression output.

Figure 6.4: Summary Output

Regression Statistics	
Multiple R	0.7800
R Square	0.6084
Adjusted R Square	0.5692
Standard error	2.3436
Observations	12

Anova

	df	SS	MS	F	Significance F
Regression	1	85.3243	85.3243	15.5345	0.0028
Residual	10	54.9257	5.4926		
Total	11	140.25			

	Coefficients	Standard Error	t Stat	P-value*	Lower 95%	Upper 95%
Intercept	10.583643	2.1796	4.8558	0.0007	5.7272	15.4401
DLH	0.563197	0.1429	3.9414	0.0028	0.2448	0.8816

*The P-value for X Variable = .0028 indicates that we have a 0.28% chance that the true value of the variable coefficient is equal to 0, implying a high level of accuracy about the estimated value of 0.563197.

The result shows:

Y' = 10.58364 + 0.563197 X (in the form of Y' = a + bX)

with:

R-squared (R^2 = 0.608373 = 60.84%)

All of the above are the same as the ones manually obtained.

Chapter Summary

Cost/managerial accountants analyze cost behavior for cost-volume-profit analysis, for appraisal of managerial performance, for flexible budgeting, and to make short-term choice decisions. We have looked at three types of cost behavior—variable, fixed and mixed. We illustrated two popular methods of separating mixed costs in their variable and fixed components: the high-low method and regression analysis. Heavy emphasis was placed on the use of simple and multiple regressions.

Chapter 7

Budgeting for Profit Planning and Financial Modeling

A comprehensive (master) budget is a formal statement of management's expectation regarding sales, expenses, volume and other financial transactions of an organization for the coming period. Simply put, a budget is a set of pro forma (projected or planned) financial statements. It consists basically of a pro forma income statement, pro forma balance sheet and cash budget.

A budget is a tool for both planning and control. At the beginning of the period, the budget is a plan or standard; at the end of the period it serves as a control device to help management measure its performance against the plan so that future performance may be improved.

It is important to realize that with the aid of computer technology, budgeting can be used as an effective device for evaluation of what-if scenarios. This way management should be able to move toward finding the best course of action among various alternatives through simulation.

If management does not like what they see on the budgeted financial statements in terms of various financial ratios such as liquidity, activity (turnover), leverage, profit margin and market value ratios, they can always alter their contemplated decision and planning set.

Types of Budgets

The budget is classified broadly into two categories:

1. operating budget, reflecting the results of operating decisions
2. financial budget, reflecting the financial decisions of the firm

The operating budget consists of:

- sales budget
- production budget
- direct materials budget
- direct labor budget
- factory overhead budget
- selling and administrative expense budget
- pro forma income statement

The financial budget consists of:

- cash budget
- pro forma balance sheet

The major steps in preparing the budget are:

1. Prepare a sales forecast.
2. Determine expected production volume.
3. Estimate manufacturing costs and operating expenses.
4. Determine cash flow and other financial effects.
5. Formulate projected financial statements.

Figure 7.1 shows a simplified diagram of the various parts of the comprehensive (master) budget, the master plan of the company.

Illustration

To illustrate how all these budgets are put together, we will focus on a manufacturing company called the Putnam Company, which produces and markets a single product. We will make the following assumptions:

- The company uses a single material and one type of labor in the manufacture of the product.
- It prepares a master budget on a quarterly basis.
- Work in process inventories at the beginning and end of the year are negligible and are ignored.
- The company uses a single cost driver—direct labor hours (DLH)—as the allocation base for assigning all factory overhead costs to the product.

Figure 7.1: Comprehensive (Master) Budget

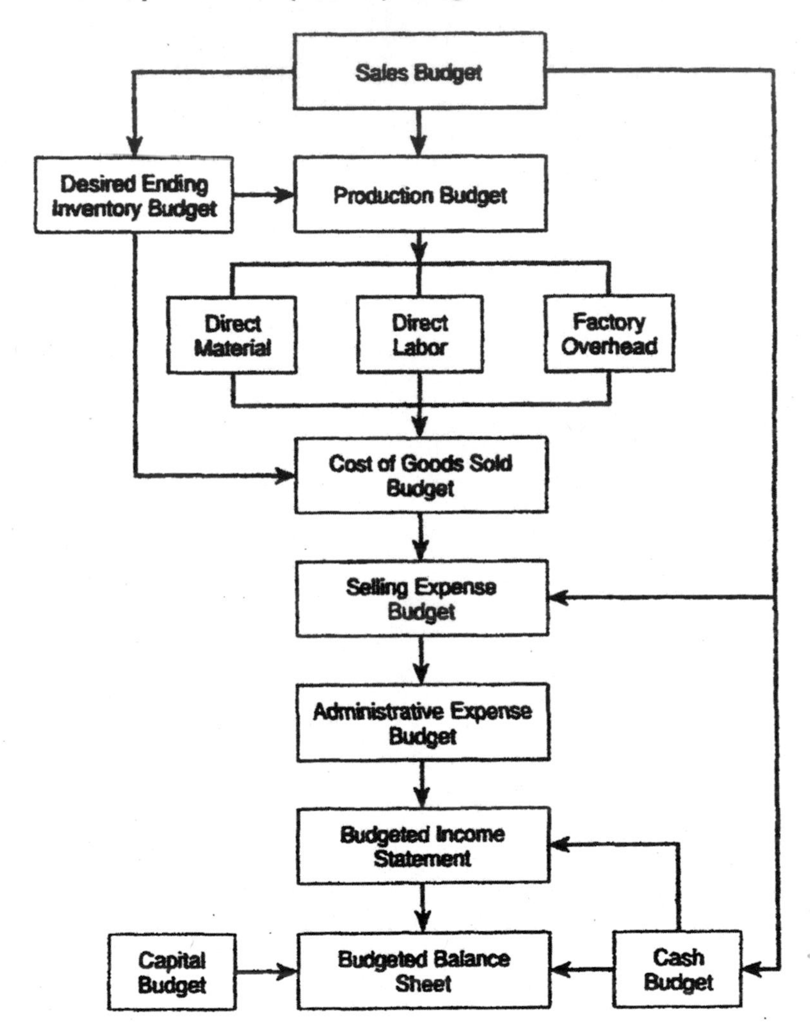

The Sales Budget

The sales budget is the starting point in preparing the master budget, since estimated sales volume influences nearly all other items appearing throughout the master budget. The sales budget should show total sales in quantity and value. The expected total sales can be break-even or target income sales or projected sales. It may be analyzed further by product, by territory, by customer and, of course, by seasonal pattern of expected sales.

Generally, the sales budget includes a computation of expected cash collections from credit sales, which will be used later for cash budgeting.

Schedule I

THE PUTNAM COMPANY

Sales Budget

For the Year Ended December 31, 20B

	Quarter				
	1	2	3	4	Year as a Whole
Expected sales in units*	1,000	1,800	2,000	1,200	6,000
Unit sales price*	x $150	x $150	x $150	x $150	x $150
Total sales	$150,000	$270,000	$300,000	$180,000	$900,000

*Given.

Schedule of Expected Cash Collections

Accounts receivable, 12/31/20A	100,000+				$100,000
1st quarter sales ($150,000)	60,000++	$90,000+++			150,000
2d quarter sales ($270,000)		108,200	$162,000		270,000
3d quarter sales ($300,000)			120,000	$180,000	300,000
4th quarter sales ($180,000)				72,000	72,000
Total cash collections	$160,000	$198,000	$282,000	$252,000	$892,000

+ All of the $100,000 accounts receivable balance is assumed to be collectible in the first quarter.

++ 40 percent of a quarter's sales are collected in the quarter of sale.

+++ 60 percent of a quarter's sales are collected in the quarter following.

Monthly Cash from Customers

Frequently, there are time lags between monthly sales made on account and their related monthly cash collections. For example, in any month, credit sales are collected as follows: 15 percent in month of sale, 60 percent in the following month, 24 percent in the month after and the remaining 1 percent are uncollectible.

	April-Actual	May-Actual	June-Budgeted	July-Budgeted
Credit sales	$320	200	300	280

The budgeted cash receipts for June and July are computed as follows:

For June:

From April sales	$320 x .24	$ 76.80
From May sales	200 x .6	120.00
From June sales	300 x .15	45.00
Total budgeted collections in June		$241.80

For July:

From May sales	$200 x .24	$ 48
From June sales	300 x .6	180
From July sales	280 x .15	42
Total budgeted collections in July		$270

The Production Budget

After sales are budgeted, the production budget can be determined. The production budget is a statement of the output by product and is generally expressed in units. It should take into account the sales budget, plant capacity, whether stocks are to be increased or decreased and outside purchases. The number of units expected to be manufactured to meet budgeted sales and inventory requirements is set forth in the production budget.

Expected production volume = Planned sales + Desired ending inventory – Beginning inventory

The production budget is illustrated as follows:

Schedule 7.2: The Putnam Company
Production Budget: For the Year Ended December 31, 20B

	Quarter				
	1	2	3	4	Year as a Whole
Planned sales (Schedule 1)	1,000	1,800	2,000	1,200	6,000
Desired ending inventory*	180	200	120	300**	300
Total Needs	1,180	2,000	2,120	1,500	6,300
Less: Beginning inventory	200**	180***	200	120	200
Units to be produced	980	1,820	1,920	1,380	6,100

* 10 percent of the next quarter's sales. (For example, 180 = 10% x 1,800).

** Given.

*** The same as the previous quarter's ending inventory.

Inventory Purchases-Merchandising Firm

Putnam Company is a manufacturing firm, so it prepares a production budget, as shown in Schedule 2. If it were a merchandising (retailing or wholesaling) firm, then instead of a production budget, it would develop a merchandise purchase budget showing the amount of goods to be purchased from its suppliers during the period. The merchandise purchase budget is in the same basic format as the production budget, except that it shows goods to be purchased rather than goods to be produced, as shown below:

Budgeted cost of goods sold (in units or dollars)	$500,000
Add: Desired ending merchandise inventory	120,000
Total needs	$620,000
Less: Beginning merchandise inventory	(90,000)
Required purchases (in units or in dollars)	$530,000

The Direct Material Budget

When the level of production has been computed, a direct material budget should be constructed to show how much material will be required for production and how much material must be purchased to meet this production requirement. The purchase will depend on both expected usage of materials and inventory levels. The formula for computation of the purchase is:

> Purchase in units = Usage + Desired ending material inventory units - Beginning inventory units

The direct material budget is usually accompanied by a computation of expected cash payments for materials.

Schedule 7.3: The Putnam Company
Direct Material Budget For the Year Ended December 31, 20B

	Quarter				
	1	2	3	4	Year as a Whole
Units to be produced (Sch.2)	980	1,820	1,920	1,380	6,100
Material needs per unit (lbs)*	x 2	x 2	x 2	x 2	x 2
Production needs (usage)	1,960	3,640	3,840	2,760	12,200
Desired ending inventory of materials**	910	960	690	520***	520
Total needs	2,870	4,600	4,530	3,280	12,720
Less: Beginning inventory of materials	490**	910****	960	690	490
Materials to be purchased	2,380	3,690	3,570	2,590	12,230
Unit price*	x $5	x $5	x $5	x $5	x $5
Purchase cost	$11,900	$18,450	$17,850	$12,950	$61,150

* Given.

** 25 percent of the next quarter's units needed for production. For example, the 2nd quarter production needs are 3,640 lbs. Therefore, the desired ending inventory for the 1st quarter would be 25% x 3,640 lbs. = 910 lbs. Also note: 490 lbs = 25% x 1,960 = 490 lbs.

*** Assume that the budgeted production needs in lbs. for the 1st quarter of 20C = 2,080 lbs. So, 25% x 2,080 lbs. = 520 lbs.

**** The same as the prior quarter's ending inventory.

Schedule of Expected Cash Disbursements

Accounts payable, 12/31/20A	6,275+				$6,275
1st quarter purchases ($11,900)	5,950++	5,950++			11,900
2d quarter purchases ($18,450)		9,225	9,225		18,450
3d quarter purchases ($17,850)			8,925	8,925	17,850
4th quarter purchases ($12,950)				6,475	6,475
Total disbursements	$12,225	$15,175	$18,150	$15,400	$60,950

\+ All of the $6,275 accounts payable balance (from the balance sheet, 20A) is assumed to be paid in the first quarter.

++ 50 percent of a quarter's purchases are paid for in the quarter of purchase; the remaining 50 percent are paid for in the following quarter.

The Direct Labor Budget

The production requirements as set forth in the production budget also provide the starting point for the preparation of the direct labor budget. To compute direct labor requirements, expected production volume for each period is multiplied by the number of direct labor hours required to produce a single unit. The direct labor hours to meet production requirements are then multiplied by the (standard) direct labor cost per hour to obtain budgeted total direct labor costs.

Schedule 4: The Putnam Company

Direct Labor Budget

For the Year Ended December 31, 20B

	Quarter				
	1	2	3	4	Year as a Whole
Units to be produced (Sch.2)	980	1,820	1,920	1,380	6,100
Direct labor hours per unit*	x 5	x 5	x 5	x 5	x 5
Total hours	4,900	9,100	9,600	6,900	30,500
Direct labor cost per hour*	x $10	x $10	x $10	x $10	x $10
Total direct labor cost	$49,000	$91,000	$96,000	$69,000	$305,000

*Both are given.

The Factory Overhead Budget

The factory overhead budget should provide a schedule of all manufacturing costs other than direct materials and direct labor. We must remember that depreciation does not entail a cash outlay and therefore must be deducted from the total factory overhead in computing cash disbursement for factory overhead.

To illustrate the factory overhead budget, we will assume that

- Total factory overhead budgeted = \$18,300 fixed (per quarter), plus \$2 per hour of direct labor. This is one example of a cost-volume (or flexible budget) formula ($y = a + bx$), developed via the least-squares method with a high R^2.
- Depreciation expenses are \$4,000 each quarter.
- Overhead costs involving cash outlays are paid for in the quarter incurred.

Schedule 5: The Putnam Company

Factory Overhead Budget

For the Year Ended December 31, 20B

	Quarter				
	1	2	3	4	Year as a Whole
Budgeted direct labor hours (Schedule 4)	4,900	9,100	9,600	6,900	30,500
Variable overhead rate	x $2	x $2	x $2	x $2	x $2
Variable overhead budgeted	9,800	18,200	19,200	13,800	61,000
Fixed overhead budgeted	18,300	18,300	18,300	18,300	73,200
Total budgeted overhead	28,100	36,500	37,500	32,100	134,200
Less: Depreciation*	4,000	4,000	4,000	4,000	16,000
Cash disbursements for factory overhead	$24,100	$32,500	$33,500	$28,100	$118,200

* Depreciation does not require a cash outlay.

The Ending Finished Goods Inventory Budget

The ending finished goods inventory budget provides us with the information required for the construction of budgeted financial statements. After completing Schedules 1-5, sufficient data will have been generated to compute the per-unit manufacturing cost of finished product. This computation is required for two reasons: to help compute the cost of goods sold on the budgeted income statement and to give the dollar value of the ending finished goods inventory to appear on the budgeted balance sheet.

Schedule 6: The Putnam Company
Ending Finished Goods Inventory Budget

For the Year Ended December 31, 20B

Ending Inventory Units	Unit Product Cost	Total
300 units (Sch. 2)	$82*	$24,600

*The unit product cost of $82 is computed as follows:

	Unit Cost	Units	Total
Direct materials	$ 5 per lbs.	2 pounds	$10
Direct labor	10 per hr.	5 hours	50
Factory overhead**	4.40 per hr.	5 hours	22
Unit product cost			$82

** Predetermined factory overhead applied rate = Budgeted annual factory overhead/budgeted annual activity units = $134,200/30,500 DLH = $4.40 (see Chapter 3; Accumulation of Costs – Job Order Costing).

The Selling and Administrative Expense Budget

The selling and administrative expense budget lists the operating expenses involved in selling the products and in managing the business. Just as in the case of the factory overhead budget, this budget can be developed using the coat-volume (flexible budget) formula in the form of y = a + bx.

If the number of expense items is very large, separate budgets may be needed for the selling and administrative functions.

Schedule 7: The Putnam Company

Selling and Administrative Expense Budget For the Year Ended December 31, 20B

	Quarter				
	1	2	3	4	Year as a Whole
Expected sales in units	1,000	1,800	2,000	1,200	6,000
Variable selling and administrative expense per unit*	x $3	x $3	x $3	x $3	x $3
Budgeted variable expense	3,000	5,400	6,000	3,600	18,000
Fixed selling and administrative expense**:					
Advertising	20,000	20,000	20,000	20,000	80,000
Insurance		12,600			12,600
Office salaries	40,000	40,000	40,000	40,000	160,000
Taxes				7,400	7,400
Total budgeted selling and administrative expenses***	$63,000	$78,000	$66,000	$71,000	$278,000

* Assumed. It includes sales agents' commissions, shipping, and supplies.

** Scheduled to be paid.

*** Paid for in the quarter incurred.

The Cash Budget

The cash budget is prepared for the purpose of cash planning and control. It presents the expected cash inflow and outflow for a designated time period. The cash budget helps management keep cash balances in reasonable relationship to its needs. It aids in avoiding unnecessary idle cash and possible cash shortages. The cash budget consists typically of four major sections:

1. The cash receipts section, which is cash collections from customers and other cash receipts such as royalty income and investment income.
2. The cash disbursements section, which comprises all cash payments made by purpose.
3. The cash surplus or deficit section, which simply shows the difference between the total cash available and the total cash needed including a minimum cash balance if required. If there is surplus cash, loans may be repaid or temporary investments made.
4. The financing section, which provides a detailed account of the borrowings, repayments, and interest payments expected during the budgeting period.

Schedule 8

To illustrate, we will make the following assumptions:

- ◆ Putnam Company has an open line of credit with its bank, which can be used as needed to bolster the cash position.
- ◆ The company desires to maintain a $10,000 minimum cash balance at the end of each quarter. Therefore, borrowing must be sufficient to cover the cash shortfall and to provide for the minimum cash balance of $10,000
- ◆ All borrowings and repayments must be in multiples of $1,000 amounts, and interest is 10 percent per annum.
- ◆ Interest is computed and paid on the principal as the principal is repaid.
- ◆ All borrowings take place at the beginning of a quarter, and all repayments are made at the end of a quarter.
- ◆ No investment option is allowed in this example. The loan is self-liquidating in the sense that the borrowed money is used to obtain resources that are combined for sale, and the proceeds from sales are used to pay back the loan.

Note: To be useful for cash planning and control, the cash budget must be prepared on a monthly basis.

Cash balance, beginning
Add receipts:
Total cash available before financing (a)
Deduct disbursements:
Total cash disbursements (b)
+ Minimum cash balance desired
Total cash needed (c)
Cash surplus or deficit (a) – (c)
Financing:
Borrowing (at beginning)
Repayment (at end)
Interest
Total effects of financing (d)
Cash balance, ending [(a) – (b) + (d)]

The Putnam Company: Cash Budget For the Year Ended December 31, 20B

	From Schedule	Quarter 1	2	3	4	Year a Whole
Cash balance, beginning		$19,000*	10,675	10,000	10,350	19,000
Add: Receipts:						
Collections from customers	I	160,000	198,000	282,000	252,000	892,000
Total cash available	(a)	179,000	208,675	292,000	262,350	911,000
Less: Disbursements:						
Direct materials	3	12,225	15,175	18,150	15,400	60,950
Direct labor	4	49,000	91,000	96,000	69,000	305,000
Factory overhead	5	24,100	32,500	33,500	28,100	118,200
Selling and Admin.	7	63,000	78,000	66,000	71,000	278,000
Equipment purchase	Given	30,000	12,000	0	0	42,000
Dividends	Given	5,000	5,000	5,000	5,000	20,000
Income tax	10	15,000	15,000	15,000	15,000	60,000
Total disbursements (b)		198,325	248,675	233,650	203,500	884,150
Minimum cash balance		10,000	10,000	10,000	10,000	10,000
Total cash needed (c)		208,325	258,675	243,650	213,500	894,150
Cash surplus (deficit) (a) – (c)		(29,325)	(50,000)	48,350	48,850	16,850
Financing:						
Borrowing		30,000**	50,000	0	0	80,000
Repayment		0	0	(45,000)	(35,000)	(80,000)
Interest		0	0	(3,000)***	(2,625)+	(5,625)
Total effects of financing (d)		30,000	50,000	(48,000)	(37,625)	(5,625)
Cash balance, ending [(a) – (b) + (d)]	$10,675			10,350	21,225	$21,225

* $19,000 (from the balance sheet 20A).

** The company desires to maintain a $10,000 minimum cash balance at the end of each quarter. Therefore, borrowing must be sufficient to cover the cash shortfall of $19,325 and to provide for the minimum cash balance of $10,000, for a total of $29,325.

*** The interest payments relate only to the principal being repaid at the time it is repaid. For example, the interest in quarter 3 relates only to the interest due on the $30,000 principal being repaid from quarter 1 borrowing and on the $15,000 principal being repaid from quarter 2 borrowing. Total interest being paid is $3,000, shown as follows:

$30,000 x 10% x 3/4 = $2,250

$15,000 x 10% x 2/4 = 750

\+ $35,000 x 10% x 3/4 = $2,625

The Budgeted Income Statement

The budgeted income statement summarizes the various component projections of revenue and expenses for the budgeting period. However, for control purposes the budget can be divided into quarters or even months depending on the need.

Schedule 9: The Putnam Company

Budgeted Income Statement

For the Year Ended December 31, 20B

	From Schedule		
Sales (6,000 units @ $150)	1		$900,000
Less: Cost of goods sold			
Beginning finished goods inventory	10	$ 16,400	
Add: Cost of goods manufactured (6,100 units @$82)	6	500,200	
Cost of goods available for sale		516,600	
Less: Ending finished goods inventory	6	(24,600)	
			$492,000
Gross margin			$408,000
Less: Selling and administrative expense	7		278,000
Operating income			130,000
Less: Interest expense	8		5,625
Net income before taxes			124,375
Less: Income taxes			60,000
Net income after taxes			$64,375

*Estimated

The Budgeted Balance Sheet

The budgeted balance sheet is developed by beginning with the balance sheet for the year just ended and adjusting it, using all the activities that are expected to take place during the budgeting period. Some of the reasons why the budgeted balance sheet must be prepared are:

- It could disclose some unfavorable financial conditions that management might want to avoid.

- It serves as a final check on the mathematical accuracy of all the other schedules.
- It helps management perform a variety of ratio calculations.
- It highlights future resources and obligations.

We can construct the budgeted balance sheet by using :

- the December, 20A balance sheet (Schedule 10);
- the cash budget (Schedule 8); and
- the budgeted income statement (Schedule 9).

Putnam's budgeted balance sheet for December 31, 20B, is presented below. Supporting calculations of the individual statement accounts are also provided.

Schedule 10: The Putnam Company

To illustrate, we will use the following balance sheet for the year 20A.

Balance Sheet December 31, 20A		
Assets		
Current assets:		
Cash	$ 19,000	
Accounts receivable	100,000	
Materials inventory (490 lbs.)	2,450	
Finished goods inventory (200 units)	16,400	
Total current assets		$137,850
Plant and equipment:		
Land	30,000	
Buildings and equipment	250,000	
Accumulated depreciation	(74,000)	
Plant and equipment, net		206,000
Total assets		$343,850
Liabilities and Stockholders' Equity		
Current liabilities		
Accounts payable (raw materials)	$ 6,275	
Income tax payable	60,000	
Total current liabilities		$66,275
Stockholders' equity:		
Common stock, no par	$200,000	
Retained earnings	77,575	
Total stockholders' equity		277,575
Total liabilities and stockholders' equity		$343,850

THE PUTNAM COMPANY

Balance Sheet December 31, 20B

Assets			
Cash	$ 21,225	(a)	
Accounts receivable	108,000	(b)	
Materials inventory (520 lbs.)	2,600	(c)	
Finished goods inventory (300 units)	24,600	(d)	
Total current assets			$156,425
Plant and equipment:			
Land	30,000	(e)	
Buildings and equipment	292,000	(f)	
Accumulated depreciation	(90,000)	(g)	
Plant and equipment, net			232,000
Total assets			$388,425
Liabilities and Stockholders' Equity			
Current liabilities			
Accounts payable (raw materials)	$ 6,475	(h)	
Income tax payable	60,000	(i)	
Total current liabilities			$66,475
Stockholders' equity:			
Common stock, no par	$200,000	(j)	
Retained earnings	121,950	(k)	
Total stockholders' equity			321,950
Total liabilities and stockholders' equity			$388,425

Supporting computations:

a. From Schedule 8 (cash budget).

b. $100,000 (Accounts receivable, 12/31/20A) + $900,000 (Credit sales from Schedule 1) - $892,000(Collections from Schedule 1) = $108,000, or 60 percent of 4th quarter credit sales, from Schedule 1 ($180,000 x 60% = $108,000).

c. Direct materials, ending inventory = 520 pounds x $ 5 = $2,600 (From Schedule 3)

d. From Schedule 6 (ending finished goods inventory budget).

e. From the 20A balance sheet and Schedule 8 (no change).

f. $250,000 (Building and Equipment, 12/31/20A) + $42,000 (purchases from Schedule 8) = $292,000.

g. $74,000 (Accumulated Depreciation, 12/31/20A) + $16,000 (depreciation expense from Schedule 5) = $90,000.

h. Note that all accounts payable relate to material purchases. $6,275 (Accounts payable, 12/31/20A) + $61,150 (credit purchases from Schedule 3) - $60,950 (payments for purchases from Schedule 3) = $6,475, or 50 percent of 4th quarter purchase = 50% ($12,950) = $6,475.

i. From Schedule 9.

j. From the 20A balance sheet and Schedule 8 (no change).

k. $77,575 (Retained earnings, 12/31/20A) + $64,375 (net income for the period, Schedule 9) – $20,000 (cash dividends from Schedule 8) = $121,950.

Some Financial Calculations

To see what kind of financial condition the Putnam Company is expected to be in for the budgeting year, a sample of financial ratio calculations are in order: (Assume 20A after-tax net income was $45,000)

	20A	20B
Current ratio:		
(Current assets/current liabilities)	$137,850/$66,275	$156,425/$66,475
	=2.08	=2.35
Return on total assets:		
(Net income after taxes/total assets)	$45,000/$343,850	$64,375/$388,425
	=13.08%	=16.57%

Sample calculations indicate that the Putnam Company is expected to have better liquidity as measured by the current ratio. Overall performance will be improved as measured by return on total assets. This could be an indication that the contemplated plan may work out well.

Financial Modeling: Computer-Based and Spreadsheet Models for Budgeting

More and more companies are developing computer-based models for financial planning and budgeting, using powerful, yet easy-to-use, financial modeling languages such as Centage's *BudgetMastro* and *Up Your Cash Flow*. The models help not only build a budget for profit planning but answer a variety of what-if scenarios. The resultant calculations provide a basis for choice among alternatives under conditions of uncertainty. Furthermore, budget modeling can also be accomplished using spreadsheet programs such as Microsoft's Excel.

Chapter Summary

A budget is a detailed quantitative plan outlining the acquisition and use of financial and other resources of an organization over some given time period. It is a tool for planning. If properly constructed, it is used as a control device. This chapter showed, step-by-step, how to formulate a master budget. The process begins with the development of a sales budget and proceeds through a number of steps that ultimately lead to the cash budget, the budgeted income statement, and the budgeted balance sheet.

Computer-based models and spreadsheet software have been utilized for budgeting in an effort to speed up the budgeting process and allow managerial accountants to investigate the effects of changes in budget assumptions.

Chapter 8

Responsibility Accounting and Cost Control through Standard Costs

Responsibility accounting is the system for collecting and reporting revenue and cost information by areas of responsibility. It operates on the premise that managers should be held responsible for their performance, the performance of their subordinates and all activities within their responsibility center. Responsibility accounting, also called profitability accounting and activity accounting, has the following advantages:

1. It facilitates delegation of decision making.
2. It helps management promote the concept of management by objective. In management by objective, managers agree on a set of goals. The manager's performance is then evaluated based on his or her attainment of these goals.
3. It provides a guide to the evaluation of performance and helps to establish standards of performance which are then used for comparison purposes.
4. It permits effective use of the concept of management by exception, which means that the manager's attention is concentrated on the important deviations from standards and budgets.

Responsibility Accounting and Responsibility Center

For an effective responsibility accounting system, the following three basic conditions are necessary:

- The organization structure must be well defined. Management responsibility and authority must go hand in hand at all levels and must be clearly established and understood.
- Standards of performance in revenues, costs and investments must be properly determined and well defined.

- The responsibility accounting reports (or performance reports) should include only items that are controllable by the manager of the responsibility center. Also, they should highlight items calling for managerial attention.

A well-designed responsibility accounting system establishes responsibility centers within the organization. A responsibility center is defined as a unit in the organization which has control over costs, revenues, and/or investment funds. Responsibility centers can be one of the following types:

Cost Center

A cost center is the unit within the organization which is responsible only for costs. Examples include production and maintenance departments of a manufacturing company. Variance analysis based on standard costs and flexible budgets would be a typical performance measure of a cost center.

Profit Center

A profit center is the unit which is held responsible for the revenues earned and costs incurred in that center. Examples might include a sales office of a publishing company, an appliance department in a retail store and an auto repair center in a department store. The contribution approach to cost allocation is widely used to measure the performance of a profit center.

Investment Center

An investment center is the unit within the organization which is held responsible for the costs, revenues and related investments made in that center. The corporate headquarters or division in a large decentralized organization would be an example of an investment center.

Figure 8.1 illustrates the manners in which responsibility accounting can be used within an organization and highlights profit and cost centers. This chapter discusses in detail how the performance of both cost and profit centers are evaluated. Performance evaluation of the investment center is reserved until Chapter 9.

Figure 8.1: Responsibility Centers

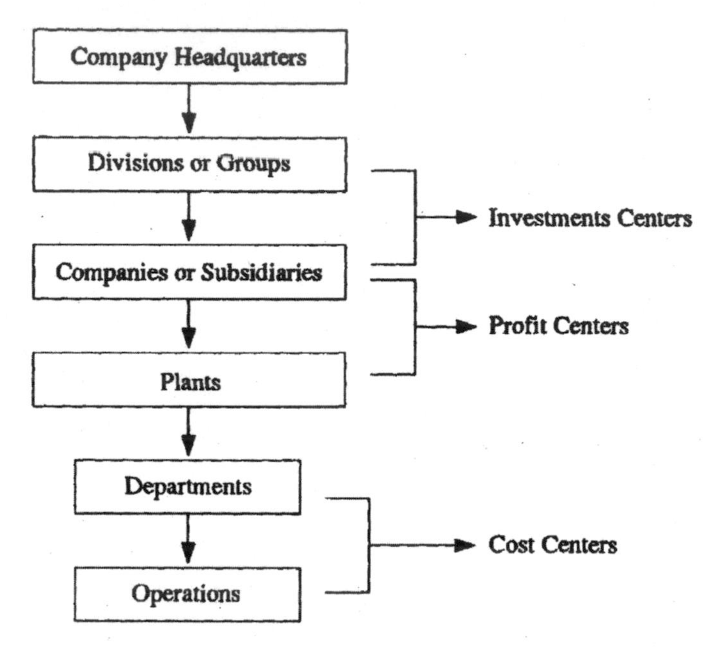

Standard Costs and Variance Analysis

One of the most important phases of responsibility accounting is establishing standard costs and evaluating performance by comparing actual costs with the standard costs. Standard costs are costs that are established in advance to serve as targets to be met and after the fact, to determine how well those targets were actually met. The standard cost is based on physical and dollar measures: It is determined by multiplying the standard quantity of an input by its standard price.

The difference between the actual costs and the standard costs, called the variance, is calculated for individual cost centers. Variance analysis is a key tool for measuring performance of a cost center. Note: A standard cost system can be used in both job-order and process costing systems to isolate variances.

The performance reports based on the analysis of variances must be prepared for each cost center, addressing the following questions:

1. Is it favorable (F) or unfavorable (U)?
2. If it is unfavorable, is it significant enough for further investigation? For example, a 5 percent over the standard is a redflag. The decision to investigate is based on the company's policy in terms of the standard plus or minus an allowable control limit. Current practice sets the control limits subjectively, based on judgment and past experience rather than any formal identification of limits. About 45 percent to 47 percent of the firms surveyed used dollar or percentage control limits.

3. If it is significant, is it controllable? For example, it may be due to a strike on the part of the supplier. A material shortage and the ensuing price hike may not be within the control of the production manager.
4. If it is controllable, then who is responsible for what portion of the total variance?
5. What are the causes for an unfavorable variance?
6. What is the remedial action to take?

The whole purpose of variance analysis is to determine what happened, what the causes are, and make sure the same thing does not happen again. The report is useful in two ways: in focusing attention on situations in need of management action and in increasing the precision of planning and control of costs. The report should be produced as part of the overall standard costing and responsibility accounting system.

Figure 8.2 takes you, step by step, through variance analysis.

Figure 8.2: Using Variance Analysis to Control Costs

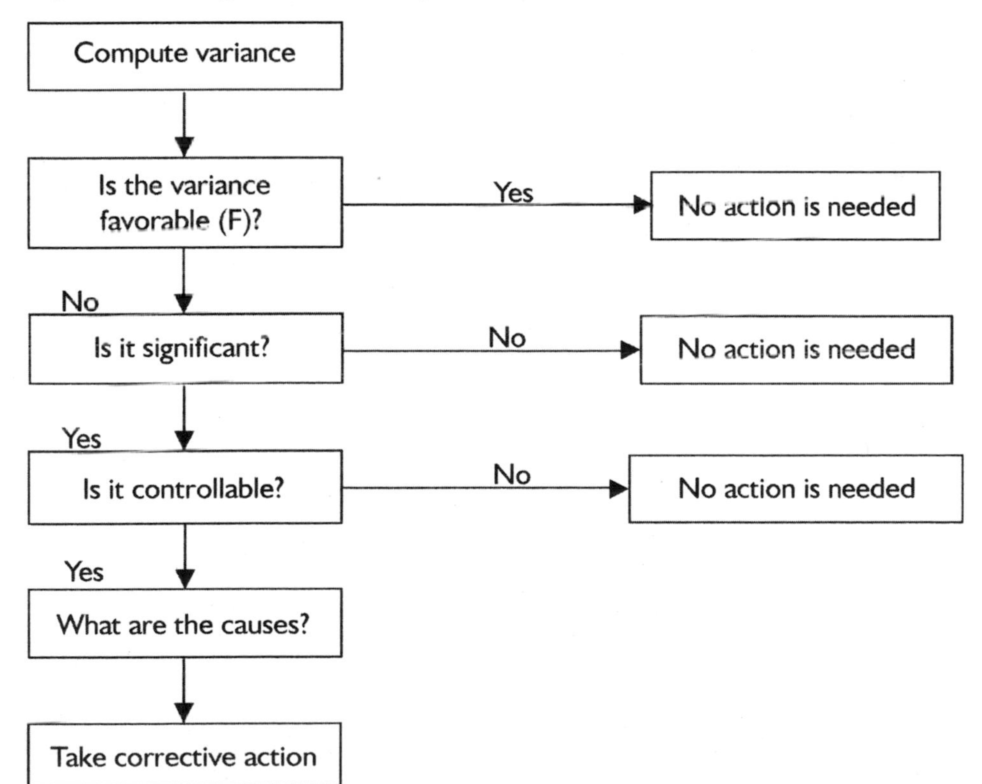

General Model for Variance Analysis

Two general types of variances can be calculated for most cost items: a price (rate, spending) variance and a quantity (usage, efficiency) variance.

The price variance is calculated as follows:

Price variance = Actual quantity * (Actual price - Standard price)
= AQ * (AP - SP)
= (AQ * AP) - (AQ * SP)
(1) (2)

The quantity variance is calculated as follows:

Quantity variance = Actual (quantity - Standard quantity) * Standard price
= (AQ - SQ) * SP
= (AQ * SP) - (SQ * SP)
(2) (3)

Figure 8.2 shows a general model (3-column model) for variance analysis that incorporates items (1), (2) and (3) from the above equations.

Figure 8.2: A General Model for Variance Analysis of Variable Manufacturing Costs

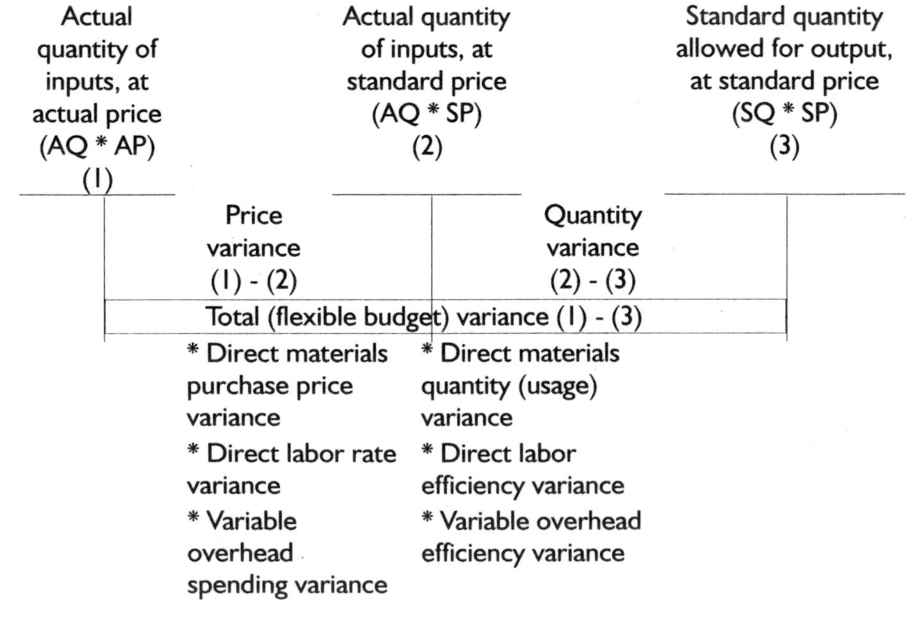

It is important to note four things:

1. A price variance and a quantity variance can be calculated for all three variable cost items—direct materials, direct labor and the variable portion of factory overhead. The variance is not called by the same name, however. For example, a price variance is called a materials price variance in the case of direct materials, but a labor rate variance in the case of direct labor and a variable overhead spending variance in the case of variable factory overhead.
2. A cost variance is unfavorable (U) if the actual price (AP) or actual quantity (AQ) exceeds the standard price (SP) or standard quantity (SQ); a variance is favorable (F) if the actual price or actual quantity is less than the standard price or standard quantity.
3. The standard quantity allowed for output—item (3)—is the key concept in variance analysis. This is the standard quantity that should have been used to produce actual output. It is computed by multiplying the actual output by the number of input units allowed.
4. Variances for fixed overhead are of questionable usefulness for control purposes, since these variances are usually beyond the control of the production department.

We will now illustrate the variance analysis for each of the variable manufacturing cost items.

Materials Variances

A materials purchase price variance is isolated at the time of purchase of the material. It is computed based on the actual quantity purchased. The purchasing department is responsible for any materials price variance that might occur. The materials quantity (usage) variance is computed based on the actual quantity used. The production department is responsible for any materials quantity variance.

Unfavorable price variances may be caused by: inaccurate standard prices, inflationary cost increases, scarcity in raw material supplies resulting in higher prices and purchasing department inefficiencies. Unfavorable material quantity variances may be explained by poorly trained workers, by improperly adjusted machines or by outright waste on the production line.

Table 8.1 provides the reasons and responsible parties for unfavorable materials variance.

Table 8.1: Reasons and Responsible Parties for Unfavorable Materials Variance

Reason	Responsible Party
Overstated price paid, failure to take discounts, improper specifications, insufficient quantities, use of a lower-grade material purchased to economize on price, uneconomical size of purchase orders, failure to obtain an adequate supply of a needed variety, purchase at an irregular time, or sudden and unexpected purchase required	Purchasing
Poor mix of materials, poorly trained workers, improperly adjusted machines, substitution of nonstandard materials, poor production scheduling, poor product design or production technique, lack of proper tools or machines, carelessness in not returning excess materials to storeroom, or unexpected volume changes	Production manager
Failure to detect defective goods	Receiving
Inefficient labor, poor supervision, or waste on the production line	Foreman
Inaccurate standard price	Budgeting
Excessive transportation charges or too small a quantity purchased	Traffic management
Insufficient quantity bought because of a lack of funds	Financial

Example I

Mighty Kings Corporation uses a standard cost system. The standard variable costs for product J are as follows:

Materials: two pounds per unit at $3 per pound ($6 per unit of product J)

Labor: one hour per unit at $5 per hour ($5 unit of product J)

Variable overhead: one hour per unit at $3 per hour ($3 per unit of product J)

During March, 25,000 pounds of material were purchased for $74,750 and 20,750 pounds of material were used in producing 10,000 units of finished product. Direct labor costs incurred were $49,896 (10,080 direct labor hours) and variable overhead costs incurred were $34,776.

Using the general model (3-column model), the materials variances are shown in Figure 8.3.

Figure 8.3: Materials Variances

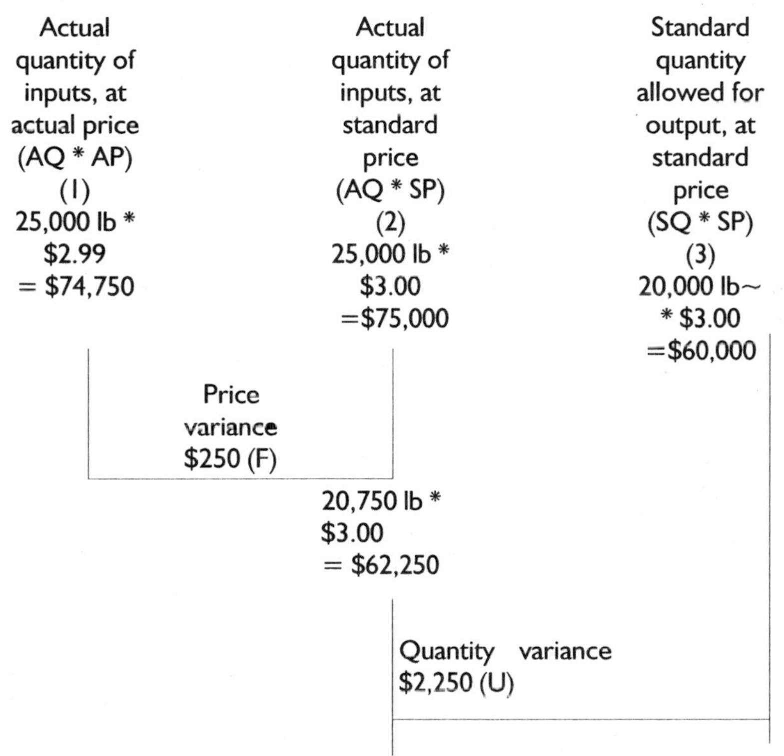

~ 10,000 units actually produced * two pounds allowed per unit = 20,000 pounds.

It is important to note that the amount of materials purchased (25,000 pounds) differs from the amount of materials used in production (20,750 pounds). The materials purchase price variance was computed using 25,000 pounds purchased, whereas the materials quantity (usage) variance was computed using the 20,750 pounds used in production. A total variance cannot be computed because of the difference.

Alternatively, we can compute the materials variances as follows:

Materials purchase price variance = AQ (AP - SP)

= (AQ * AP) - (AQ * SP)

= (25,000 pounds) ($2.99 - $3.00)

= $74,750 - $75,000

= $250 (F)

Materials quantity (usage) variance = (AQ - SQ) SP

= (20,750 pounds - 20,000 pounds) ($3.00)

= $62,250 - $60,000

= $2,250 (U)

Labor Variances

Labor variances are isolated when labor is used for production. They are computed in a manner similar to the materials variances, except that in the 3-column model the terms efficiency and rate are used in place of the terms quantity and price. The production department is responsible for both the prices paid for labor services and the quantity of labor services used. Therefore, the production department must explain why any labor variances occur.

Unfavorable rate variances may be explained by an increase in wages or the use of labor commanding higher wage rates than contemplated. Unfavorable efficiency variances may be explained by poor supervision, poor quality workers, poor quality of materials requiring more labor time, machine breakdowns and employee unrest. Table 8.2 provides the reasons and responsible parties for an unfavorable labor variance.

Table 8.2: Reason and Responsible Parties for an Unfavorable Labor Variance

Reason	Responsible Party
Use of overpaid or excessive number of workers	Production manager or union contract
Poor job descriptions or excessive wages	Personnel
Overtime and poor scheduling of production	Production planning
Poor quality workers or poor training	Personnel or training
Inadequate supervision, inefficient flow of materials, wrong mixture of labor for a given job, inferior tools or idle time from production delays	Foreman
Employee unrest	Personnel or Foreman
Improper functioning of equipment	Maintenance
Insufficient material supply or poor quality	Purchasing

Example 2

Using the same data given in Example 1, the labor variances can be calculated as shown in Figure 8.4.

Figure 8.4: Labor Variances

Actual quantity of inputs, at actual price (AH * AR) (1)		Actual quantity of inputs, at standard price (AH * SR) (2)		Standard quantity allowed for output, at standard price (SH * SR) (3)
10,080 h * $4.95 = $49,896		10,080 h * $5.00 = $50,400		10,000 h~ * $5.00 = $50,000
	Price variance (1) - (2) $504 (F)		Efficiency variance (2) - (3) $400 (U)	
		Total variance $104 (F)		

~ 10,000 units actually produced * one hour (h) allowed per unit = 10,000 hours.

Note: The symbols AQ, SQ, AP and SP have been changed to AH, SH, AR and SR to reflect the terms hour and rate.

Alternatively, we can calculate the labor variances as follows:

- Labor rate variance = AH (AR - SR)
  = (AH * AR) - (AH * SR)
  = (10,080 hours) ($4.95 - $5.00)
  = $49,896 - $50,400
  = $504 (F)
- Labor efficiency variance = (AH - SH) SR
  = (10,080 hours - 10,000 hours) * $5.00
  = $50,400 - $50,000
  = $400 (U)

Variable Overhead Variances

The variable overhead variances are computed in a way very similar to the labor variances. The production department is usually responsible for any variable overhead variance. Unfavorable variable overhead spending variances may be caused by a large number of factors: acquiring supplies for a price different from the standard, using more supplies than expected, waste and theft of supplies. Unfavorable variable overhead efficiency variances might be caused by such factors as: poorly trained workers, poor-quality materials, faulty equipment, work interruptions, poor production scheduling, poor supervision, employee unrest and so on.

When variable overhead is applied using direct labor hours, the efficiency variance will be caused by the same factors that cause the labor efficiency variance. However, when variable overhead is applied using machine hours, inefficiency in machinery will cause a variable overhead efficiency variance.

Example 3

Using the same data given in Example 1, the variable overhead variances can be computed as shown in Figure 8.5.

Alternatively, we can compute the variable overhead variances as follows:

Variable overhead spending variance = AH (AR - SR)

= (AH * AR) - (AH * SR)

= (10,080 hours) ($3.45 - $3.00)

= $34,776 - $30,240

= $4,536 (U)

Variable overhead efficiency variance = (AH - SH) SR

= (10,080 hours - 10,000 hours) * $3.00

= $30,240 - $30,000

= $240 (U)

Figure 8.5: Variable Overhead Variances

Actual hours of inputs, at actual price (AH * AR) (1)		Actual hours of inputs, at standard price (AH * SR) (2)		Standard hours allowed for output, at standard rate (SH * SR) (3)
10,080 h * $3.45 = $34,776		10,080 h * $3.00 = $30,240		110,000 h# * $3.00 = $30,000
	Spending variance (1) - (2) $4,536 (U)		Efficiency variance (2) - (3) $240 (U)	
Total variance $4,776 (U)				

10,000 units actually produced * one hour (h) allowed per unit = 10,000 hours.

Flexible Budgets and Performance Reports

A flexible budget is a tool that is extremely useful in cost control. In contrast to a static budget, which was discussed in Chapter 8, the flexible budget is characterized as follows:

1. It is geared toward a range of activity rather than a single level of activity.
2. It is dynamic in nature rather than static. By using the cost-volume formula (or flexible budget formula), a series of budgets can be easily developed for various levels of activity.

The static (fixed) budget is geared for only one level of activity and has problems in cost control. Flexible budgeting distinguishes between fixed and variable costs, thus allowing for a budget which can be automatically adjusted (via changes in variable cost totals) to the particular level of activity actually attained. Thus, variances between actual costs and budgeted costs are adjusted for volume ups and downs before differences due to price and quantity factors are computed.

The primary use of the flexible budget is to accurately measure performance by comparing actual costs for a given output with the budgeted costs for the same level of output.

Example 5

To illustrate the difference between the static budget and the flexible budget, assume that the Assembly Department of Omnis Industries, Inc. is budgeted to produce 6,000 units during June. Assume further that the company was able to produce only 5,800 units. The budget for direct labor and variable overhead costs is as follows:

Omnis Industries, Inc.

The Direct Labor and Variable Overhead Budget

Assembly Department
For the Month of June

Budgeted production	6,000 units
Actual production	5,800 units
Direct labor	$39,000
Variable overhead costs:	
Indirect labor	6,000
Supplies	900
Repairs	300
	$46,200

If a static budget approach is used the performance report will appear as follows:

Omnis Industries, Inc.

Direct Labor and Variable Overhead

Static Budget Versus Actual
Assembly Department
For the Month of June

	Budget	Actual*	Variance (U or F)**
Production in units	6,000	5,800	200U
Direct labor	$39,000	$38,500	$500F
Variable overhead costs:			
Indirect labor	6,000	5,950	50F
Supplies	900	870	30F
Repairs	300	295	5F
	$46,200	$45,615	$585F

* Given.

** A variance represents the deviation of actual cost from the standard or budgeted cost. U and F stand for unfavorable and favorable, respectively.

These cost variances are useless, in that they are comparing oranges with apples. The problem is that the budget costs are based on an activity level of 6,000 units, whereas the actual costs were incurred at an activity level below this (5,800 units).

From a control standpoint, it makes no sense to try to compare costs at one activity level with costs at a different activity level. Such comparisons would make a production manager look good as long as the actual production is less than the budgeted production. Using the cost-volume formula and generating the budget based on the 5,800 actual units gives the following performance report:

Omnis Industries, Inc.

Performance Report Assembly Department

Flexible Budget Versus Actual

For the Month of June

Budgeted production		6,000 units		
Actual production		5,800 units		
	Cost-volume formula	Flexible Budget 5,800 units	Actual	Variance 5,800 units (U or F)
Direct labor	$6.50 per unit	$37,700	$38,500	$800U
Variable overhead:				
Indirect labor	1.00	5,800	5,950	150U
Supplies	0.15	870	870	0
Repairs	0.05	290	295	5U
	$7.70	$44,660	$45,615	$955U

Notice that all cost variances are unfavorable (U), as compared to the favorable cost variances on the performance report based on the static budget approach.

Fixed Overhead Variances

By definition, fixed overhead does not change over a relevant range of activity; the amount of fixed overhead per unit varies inversely with the level of production. In order to calculate variances for fixed overhead, it is necessary to determine a standard fixed overhead rate, which requires the selection of a predetermined (denominator) level of activity. This activity should be measured on the basis of standard inputs allowed. The formula is:

$$\text{Standard fixed overhead rate} = \frac{\text{Budgeted fixed overhead}}{\text{Budgeted level of activity}}$$

Total fixed overhead variance is simply under- or over-applied overhead. It is the difference between actual fixed overhead incurred and fixed overhead applied to production (generally, on the basis of standard direct labor hours allowed for actual production). Total fixed overhead variance combines fixed overhead spending (flexible-budget) variance and fixed overhead volume (capacity) variance.

(a) Fixed overhead spending (flexible-budget) variance. It is the difference between actual fixed overhead incurred and budgeted fixed overhead. This variance is not affected by the level of production. Fixed overhead, by definition, does not change with the level of activity. The spending (flexible-budget) variance is caused solely by events such as unexpected changes in prices and unforeseen repairs.

(b) Fixed overhead volume (capacity) variance. This variance results when the actual level of activity differs from the denominator activity used in determining the standard fixed overhead rate. Note that the denominator used in the formula is the expected annual activity level. Fixed overhead volume variance is a measure of the cost of failure to operate at the denominator (budgeted) activity level, and may be caused by such factors as failure to meet sales targets, idleness due to poor scheduling, and machine breakdowns. The volume variance is calculated as follows:

Fixed overhead volume variance = (Budgeted fixed overhead) - (Fixed overhead applied)

or

= (Denominator activity - Standard hours allowed) x Standard fixed overhead rate

When denominator activity exceeds standard hours allowed, the volume variance is unfavorable (U), because it is an index of less-than-denominator utilization of capacity.

It is important to note that there are no efficiency variances for fixed overhead. Fixed overhead does not change regardless of whether productive resources are used efficiently or not. For example, property taxes, insurance and factory rents are not affected by whether production is being carried on efficiently.

Figure 8.6 illustrates the relationship between the various elements of fixed overhead and the possible variances.

Figure 8.6: Fixed Overhead Variances

	Incurred: actual hours x actual rate (1)	Flexible budget based on actual hours (2)		Flexible budget based on standard hours allowed (3)	Applied (4)
3-Way analysis	Spending variance (1) - (2)		Efficiency variance (Not applicable)	Volume variance (3) - (4)	
2-Way analysis	Flexible budget variance (1) - (3)			Volume variance (3) - (4)	
	(1) - (4) Under- or over-applied				

Example 4

The Doubtfire Manufacturing Company has the following standard cost of factory overhead at a normal monthly production (denominator) volume of 1,300 direct labor hours:

Variable	$2,853
Fixed	$6,725

Fixed overhead budgeted is $6,500 per month. During the month March, the following events occurred:

(a) Actual overhead costs incurred (for 1,350 hours) were:

Variable	$2,853
Fixed	$6,725

(b) Standard hour allowed, 1,250 hours (1 hour x 1,250 units of output)

Note that:

(a) Flexible budget formula:

Variable overhead rate	$2 per direct labor hour
Fixed overhead budgeted	$6,500

(b) Standard overhead applied rates:

Variable	$2 per direct labor hour
Fixed	$5 per direct labor hour

Figure 8.7 shows all the variances for variable overhead as well as fixed overhead.

Figure 8.7: Variance Analysis for Variable Overhead and Fixed Overhead

	Incurred: actual hours x actual rate (1,350 hrs)	Flexible budget based on actual hours (1,250 hrs)	Flexible budget based on standard hours allowed (1,250hrs)	Applied (1,350hrs.)
	(1)	(2)	(3)	(4)
		$2,700(1,350 X $2)	$2,500(1,250 x $2)	
	V $2,853			$2,500
	F 6,725	6,500	6,500	6,250
	$9,578	$9,200	$9,000	$8,750

	Variance		
(3-Way)	Spending variance (1) - (2) V $153 U F 225 U $378 U	Efficiency variance (Not applicable) $200 U Not applicable $200 U	Volume variance (3) - (4) Not applicable $250 U $250 U
(2-Way)	Flexible budget variance (1) - (3) V $353 U F 225 U $578 U		Volume variance (3) - (4) Not applicable $250 U $250 U
	Under- or over-applied (1) - (4) V $353 U F 475 U $828 U		

Alternatively, fixed overhead volume variance can be calculated as follows:

Fixed overhead = (Denominator activity - Standard hours allowed)
x Volume variance x Standard fixed overhead rate
= (1,300 hours - 1,250 hours) x $5
= 50 hours x $5 = $250 U

Methods of Variance Analysis for Factory Overhead

Variance analysis for factory overhead consists of a two-, three- or four-way method of computation, depending on the significance of the variance amounts compared to the cost of analysis. These methods are indicated in Figure 8.6 and Figure 8.7.

The two-way analysis computes two variances: budget variance (sometimes called the flexible-budget or controllable variance) and volume variances, which means:

(a) Budget variance = Variable spending variance
  + Fixed spending (budget) variance
  + Variable efficiency variance

(b) Volume variance = Fixed volume variance

The three-way analysis computes three variances: spending, efficiency and volume variances.

Therefore:

(a) Spending variance = Variable spending variance + Fixed spending (budget) variance

(b) Efficiency variance = Variable efficiency variance

(c) Volume variance = Fixed volume variance

The four-way analysis includes the following:

(a) variable spending variance

(b) fixed spending (budget) variance

(c) variable efficiency variance

(d) fixed volume variance

Nonfinancial Performance Measures

Standard costs are widely used in manufacturing, service and not-for-profit organizations. The list of companies using standards as a method for controlling costs and measuring performance continues to grow. For a firm to improve, managers should encompass nonfinancial (or operational) measures as well as financial measures, especially those that track factors required for world-class status. In an automated environment, labor is a smaller proportion of product cost, often less than 5 percent. Thus, traditional labor variances are of little value to management. Also, the manufacturing process is more reliable in an automated environment, and the traditional variances tend to be minimal.

The new performance measures tend to be nonfinancial and more subjective than standard costs. Table 8.1 presents five sets of nonfinancial performance measures. They include statistics for activities such as quality control, on-time delivery, inventory, machine downtime and material waste. Measures such as quality control and delivery performance are customer oriented. These are useful performance measures in all organizations, particularly organizations in which the focus is on services, not goods. A general model for measuring the relative success of an activity compares number of successes with total activity volume. For example, delivery performance could be measured as follows.

$$\frac{\text{Number of on-time deliveries}}{\text{Total delivery made}} = \text{Delivery success rate}$$

The percentage of external failures may be monitored for quality control.

Others may be production oriented. Reducing material waste, inventory and machine downtime have been shown to improve quality and efficiency. These nonfinancial performance measures and measures of performance using standard costs are not mutually exclusive. Reducing materials waste would eliminate an unfavorable materials usage variance, for example. Measures such as inventory turnover and days of inventory can be used, however. Table 8.3 illustrates nonfinancial performance measures.

Table 8.3: Nonfinancial Performance Measures

Task	Objective
Inventory:	
Inventory levels	Decrease inventory levels
Number of inventoried items	Curtail number of different items
Quality control:	
Number of customer complaints	Reduce complaints
Number of defects	Reduce defects
Delivery performance:	
Delivery success rate	Increase on-time deliveries
Materials waste:	
Scrap and waste as a percentage of total cost	Decrease scrap and waste
Machine downtime:	
Percentage of machine downtime	Reduce downtime
Human resources:	
Turnover rate	Reduce employee turnover

Chapter Summary

Variance analysis is essential in the organization for the appraisal of all aspects of the business. This chapter was concerned with the control of cost centers through standard costs. It discussed the basic mechanics of how the two major variances—the price variance and the quantity variance—are calculated for direct materials, direct labor, variable overhead and fixed overhead. Also presented are the managerial significance of these variances. The idea of flexible budgeting was emphasized in an attempt to correctly measure the efficiency of the cost center. We noted that fixed overhead volume variance has a limited usefulness at the level of a cost center, since only top management has the power to expand or contract fixed facilities.

Chapter 9

Performance Evaluation, Transfer Pricing and Decentralization

The ability to measure performance is essential in developing management incentives and controlling the operation toward the achievement of organizational goals. A typical decentralized subunit is an investment center which is responsible for an organization's invested capital (operating assets) and the related operating income. There are two widely used measurements of performance for the investment center: the rate of return on investment (ROI) and residual income (RI).

Goods and services are often exchanged between various divisions of a decentralized organization. The transfer price is the selling price credited to the selling division and the cost charged to the buying division for an internal transfer of a good or service. The choice of transfer prices not only affects divisional performance but is also important in decisions involving make or buy, whether to buy internally or outside, and choosing between production possibilities.

Rate of Return on Investment (ROI)

ROI relates net income to invested capital. Specifically:

$$\text{ROI} = \frac{\text{Operating income}}{\text{Operating assets}}$$

Example 1

Consider the following financial data for a division:

Operating assets	$100,000
Operating income	$18,000

ROI = $18,000/$100,000 = 18%

The problem with this formula is that it only indicates how a division did and how well it fared in the company. Other than that, it has very little value from the standpoint of profit planning.

The Breakdown of ROI—Du Pont Formula

In the past, managers have tended to focus only on the margin earned and have ignored the turnover of assets. It is important to realize that excessive funds tied up in assets can be just as much of a drag on profitability as excessive expenses.

The Du Pont Corporation was the first major company to recognize the importance of looking at both margin and asset turnover in assessing the performance of an investment center. The ROI breakdown, known as the Du Pont formula, is expressed as a product of these two factors, as shown below.

$$\text{ROI} = \frac{\text{Operating Income}}{\text{Operating assets}} = \underbrace{\frac{\text{Operating income}}{\text{Sales}}}_{\text{Margin}} \times \underbrace{\frac{\text{Sales}}{\text{Operating assets}}}_{\text{Asset turnover}}$$

The Du Pont formula combines the income statement and balance sheet into this otherwise static measure of performance. Margin is a measure of profitability or operating efficiency. It is the percentage of profit earned on sales. This percentage shows how many cents attach to each dollar of sales. On the other hand, asset turnover measures how well a division manages its assets. It is the number of times by which the investment in assets turns over each year to generate sales. The breakdown of ROI is based on the thesis that the profitability of a firm is directly related to management's ability to manage assets efficiently and to control expenses effectively.

Example 2

Assume the same data as in Example 1. Also assume sales of $200,000.

$$\text{Then, ROI} = \frac{\text{Operating income}}{\text{Operating assets}} = \frac{\$18{,}000}{\$100{,}000} = 18\%$$

Alternatively:

$$\text{Margin} = \frac{\text{Operating income}}{\text{Sales}} = \frac{\$18{,}000}{\$200{,}000} = 9\%$$

$$\text{Turnover} = \frac{\text{Sales}}{\text{Operating assets}} = \frac{\$200{,}000}{\$100{,}000} = 2 \text{ times}$$

Therefore:

ROI = Margin x Turnover = 9% x 2 times

The breakdown provides a lot of insights to division managers on how to improve profitability of the investment center. Specifically, it has several advantages over the original formula for profit planning. They are:

(1) Focusing on the breakdown of ROI provides the basis for integrating many of the management concerns that influence a division's overall performance. This will help managers gain an advantage in the competitive environment.

(2) The importance of turnover as a key to overall return on investment is emphasized in the breakdown. In fact, turnover is just as important as profit margin in enhancing overall return.

(3) The importance of sales is explicitly recognized, which is not there in the original formula.

(4) The breakdown stresses the possibility of trading one off for the other in an attempt to improve the overall performance of a company. The margin and turnover complement each other. In other words, a low turnover can be made up for by a high margin; and vice versa.

Example 3

The breakdown of ROI into its two components shows that a number of combinations of margin and turnover can yield the same rate of return, as shown below:

The turnover-margin relationship and its resulting ROI are depicted in Figure 9.1

Margin	x	Turnover	= ROI
(1) 9%	x	2 times	= 18%
(2) 6	x	3	= 18
(3) 3	x	6	= 18
(4) 2	x	9	= 18

The turnover-margin relationship and its resulting ROI are depicted in Figure 9.1.

Figure 9.1: The Margin-turnover Relationship

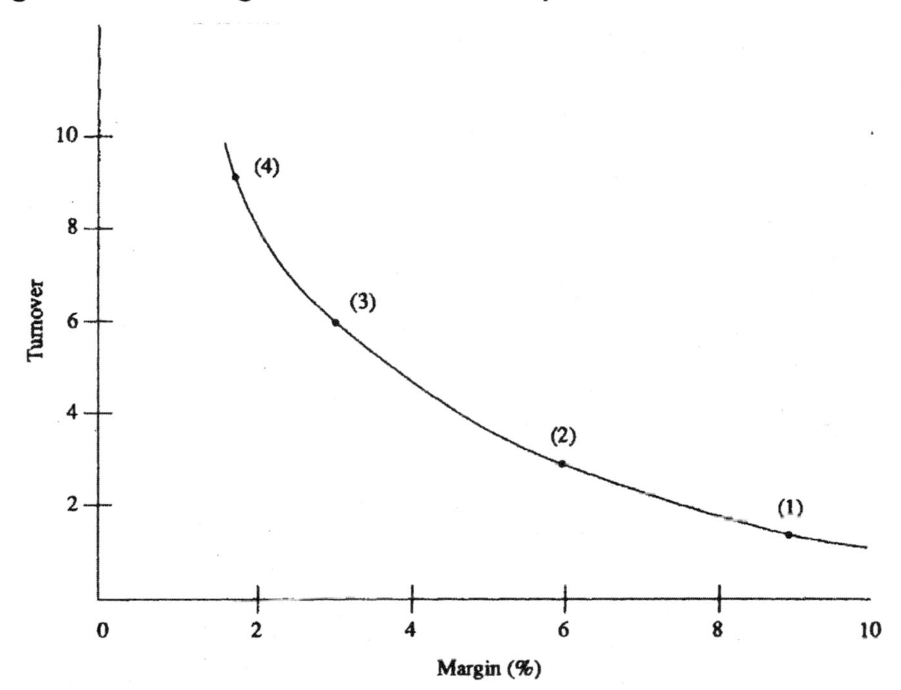

ROI and Profit Planning

The breakdown of ROI into margin and turnover gives divisional managers insight into planning for profit improvement by revealing where weaknesses exist: margin or turnover, or both. Various actions can be taken to enhance ROI. Generally, they can:

1. Improve margin;
2. improve turnover; and
3. improve both.

Alternative 1 demonstrates a popular way of improving performance. Margins may be increased by reducing expenses, raising selling prices or increasing sales faster than expenses. Some of the ways to reduce expenses are:

(a) Use less costly inputs of materials;

(b) automate processes as much as possible to increase labor productivity; and

(c) bring the discretionary fixed costs under scrutiny, with various programs either curtailed or eliminated. Discretionary fixed costs arise from annual budgeting decisions by management. Examples include advertising, research and development and management development programs. The cost-benefit analysis is called for in order to justify the budgeted amount of each discretionary program.

A division with pricing power can raise selling prices and retain profitability without losing business. Pricing power is the ability to raise prices even in poor economic times when unit sales volume may be flat and capacity may not be fully utilized. It is also the ability to pass on cost increases to consumers without attracting domestic and import competition, political opposition, regulation, new entrants or threats of product substitution. The division with pricing power must have a unique economic position. Divisions that offer unique, high-quality goods and services (where the service is more important than the cost) have this economic position.

Alternative 2 may be achieved by increasing sales while holding the investment in assets relatively constant, or by reducing assets. Some of the strategies to reduce assets are:

(a) Dispose of obsolete and redundant inventory.

(b) Devise various methods of speeding up the collection of receivables and also evaluate credit terms and policies.

(c) See if there are unused fixed assets.

(d) Use the converted assets obtained from the use of the previous methods to repay outstanding debts or repurchase outstanding issues of stock. The division may release them elsewhere to get more profit, which will improve margin as well as turnover.

Alternative 3 may be achieved by increasing sales or by any combinations of alternatives 1 and 2. Figure 9.2 shows complete details of the relationship of ROI to the underlying ratios—margin and turnover—and their components. This will help identify more detailed strategies to improve margin, turnover or both.

Example 4

Assume that management sets a 20 percent ROI as a profit target. It is currently making an 18 percent return on its investment.

$$\text{ROI} = \frac{\text{Operating income}}{\text{Operating assets}} = \frac{\text{Operating income}}{\text{Sales}} \times \frac{\text{Sales}}{\text{Operating assets}}$$

Present situation:

$$18\% = \frac{18{,}000}{200{,}000} \times \frac{200{,}000}{100{,}000}$$

The following are illustrative of the strategies which might be used (each strategy is independent of the other).

Alternative 1: Increase the margin while holding turnover constant. Pursuing this strategy would involve leaving selling prices as they are and making every effort to increase efficiency so as to reduce expenses. By doing so, expenses might be reduced by $2,000 without affecting sales and investment to yield a 20 percent target ROI, as follows:

$$20\% = \frac{20{,}000}{200{,}000} \times \frac{200{,}000}{100{,}000}$$

Alternative 2: Increase turnover by reducing investment in assets while holding net profit and sales constant. Working capital might be reduced or some land might be sold, reducing investment in assets by $10,000 without affecting sales and net income to yield the 20 percent target ROI as follows:

$$20\% = \frac{18{,}000}{200{,}000} \times \frac{200{,}000}{90{,}000}$$

Alternative 3: Increase both margin and turnover by disposing of obsolete and redundant inventories or through an active advertising campaign. For example, trimming down $5,000 worth of investment in inventories would also reduce the inventory holding charge by $1,000. This strategy would increase ROI to 20 percent.

$$20\% = \frac{19{,}000}{200{,}000} \times \frac{200{,}000}{95{,}000}$$

Excessive investment in assets is just as much of a drag on profitability as excessive expenses. In this case, cutting unnecessary inventories also helps cut down expenses of carrying those inventories, so that both margin and turnover are improved at the same time. In practice, alternative 3 is much more common than alternative 1 or 2.

Residual Income (RI)

Another approach to measuring performance in an investment centers residual income (RI). RI is the operating income, which an investment center is able to earn above some minimum rate of return on its operating assets. RI, unlike ROI, is an absolute amount of income rather than a specific rate of return. When RI is used to evaluate divisional performance, the objective is to maximize the total amount of residual income, not to maximize the overall ROI figure.

RI = Operating income - (Minimum required rate of return x Operating assets)

Example 5

In this example, assume the minimum required rate of return is 13 percent. Then the residual income of the division is:

$18,000 - (13% x $100,000) = $18,000 - $13,000 = $5,000

Figure 9.2: Relationships of Factors influencing ROI

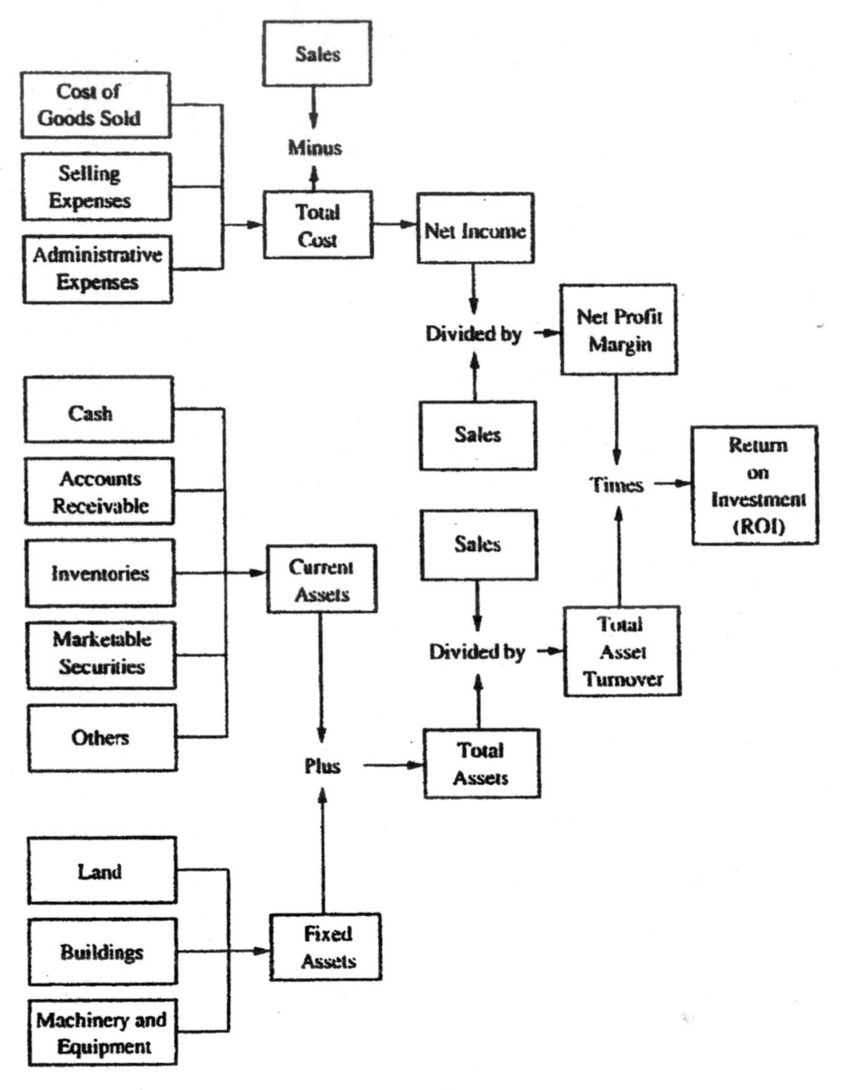

RI is regarded as a better measure of performance than ROI because it encourages investment in projects that would be rejected under ROI. A major disadvantage of RI, however, is that it cannot be used to compare divisions of different sizes. RI tends to favor the larger divisions due to the larger amount of dollars involved.

Residual Income and Economic Value Added

Residual income is better known as economic value added (EVA). Many firms are addressing the issue of aligning division managers' incentives with those of the firm by using EVA as a measure of performance. EVA encourages managers to focus on increasing the value of the company to shareholders, because EVA is the value created by a company in excess of the cost of capital for the investment base. Improving EVA can be achieved in three ways:

(a) Invest capital in high-performing projects.

(b) Use less capital.

(c) Increase profit without using more capital.

Investment Decisions under ROI and RI

The decision whether to use ROI or RI as a measure of divisional performance affects financial managers' investment decisions. Under the ROI method, division managers tend to accept only the investments whose returns exceed the division's ROI; otherwise, the division's overall ROI would decrease. Under the RI method, on the other hand, division managers would accept an investment as long as it earns a rate in excess of the minimum required rate of return. The addition of such an investment will increase the division's overall RI.

Example 6

Consider the same data given in Examples 1 and 2:

Operating assets	$100,000
Operating income	$18,000
Minimum required rate of return	13%
ROI = 18% and RI = $5,000	

Assume that the division is presented with a project that would yield 15 percent on a $10,000 investment. The division manager would not accept this project under the ROI approach since the division is already earning 18 percent. Acquiring this project will bring down the present ROI to 17.73 percent, as shown below:

	Present	New Project	Overall
Operating assets (a)	$100,000	$10,000	$110,000
Operating income (b)	18,000	1,500*	19,500
ROI (b / a)	18%	15%	17.73%

**$10,000 x 15% = $1,500*

Under the RI approach, the manager would accept the new project since it provides a higher rate than the minimum required rate of return (15 percent vs. 13 percent).

Accepting the new project will increase the overall residual income to $5,200, as shown below:

	Present	New Project	Overall
Operating assets (a)	$100,000	$10,000	$110,000
Operating income (b)	18,000	1,500	19,500
Minimum required income at 13%(c)	13,000	1,300*	14,300
RI (b-c)	$5,000	$200	$5,200

**$10,000 x 13% = $1,300*

Corporate Balanced Scorecard

A problem with just assessing performance with financial measures like profit, ROI and RI is that the financial measures are backward looking. In other words, today's financial measures tell you about the accomplishments and failures of the past. An approach to performance measurement that also focuses on what managers are doing today to create future shareholder value is the corporate balanced scorecard (CBS).

Essentially, a corporate balanced scorecard is a set of performance measures constructed for four dimensions of performance. The dimensions are:

1. financial
2. customer
3. internal processes
4. learning and growth

Having financial measures is critical even if they are backward looking. After all, they have a great affect on the evaluation of the company by shareholders and creditors. Customer measures examine the company's success in meeting customer expectations. Internal process measures examine the company's success in improving critical business processes. And learning and growth measures examine the company's success in improving its ability to adapt, innovate and grow. The customer, internal processes and learning and growth measures are generally thought to be predictive of future success (i.e., they are not backward looking).

After reviewing these measures, note how balance is achieved:

- Performance is assessed across a balanced set of dimensions (financial, customer, internal processes and innovation).
- Quantitative measures (e.g., number of defects) are balanced with qualitative measures (e.g., ratings of customer satisfaction).

- There is a balance of backward-looking measures (e.g., financial measures like growth in sales) and forward-looking measures (e.g., number of new patents as an innovation measure).

Transfer Pricing

Goods and services are often exchanged between various divisions of a decentralized organization. A major goal of transfer pricing is to enable divisions that exchange goods or services to act as independent businesses.

The question then is: What monetary values should be assigned to these exchanges or transfers? Market price? Some kind of cost? Some version of either? Unfortunately, there is no single transfer price that will please everybody—that is, top management, the selling division and the buying division-involved in the transfer. Various transfer pricing schemes are available, such as market price, cost-based price or negotiated price.

The choice of a transfer pricing policy (i.e., which type of transfer price to use) is normally decided by top management. The decision will typically include consideration of the following:

- Goal congruence. Will the transfer price promote the goals of the company as a whole? Will it harmonize the divisional goals with organizational goals?
- Performance evaluation. Will the selling division receive enough credit for its transfer of goods and services to the buying division? Will the transfer price hurt the performance of the selling division?
- Autonomy. Will the transfer price preserve autonomy; the freedom of the selling and buying division managers to operate their divisions as decentralized entities?
- Other factors such as minimization of tariffs and income taxes and observance of legal restrictions.

Transfer prices can be based on:

- market price
- cost-based price - variable or full cost
- negotiated price
- general formula

Note that the general formula is usually the sum of variable costs per unit and opportunity cost for the company as a whole (lost revenue per unit on outside sales)

Market Price

Market price is the best transfer price in the sense that it will maximize the profits of the company as a whole, if it meets the following two conditions:

- There exists a competitive market price.
- Divisions are independent of each other.

If either one of these conditions is violated, market price will not lead to an optimal economic decision for the company.

Cost-based Price – Variable or Full Cost

Cost-based transfer price, another alternative transfer pricing scheme, is easy to understand and convenient to use. But there are some disadvantages, including:

- Inefficiencies of selling divisions are passed on to the buying divisions with little incentive to control costs. The use of standard costs is recommended in such a case.
- The cost-based method treats the divisions as cost centers rather than profit or investment centers. Therefore, measures such as ROI and RI cannot be used for evaluation purposes.

The variable-cost-based transfer price has an advantage over the full cost method because in the short run it may tend to ensure the best utilization of the overall company's resources. The reason is that, in the short run, fixed costs do not change. Any use of facilities, without incidence of additional fixed costs, will increase the company's overall profits.

Negotiated Price

A negotiated price is generally used when there is no clear outside market. A negotiated price is a price agreed upon between the buying and selling divisions that reflects unusual or mitigating circumstances. This method is widely used when no intermediate market price exists for the product transferred and the selling division is assured of a normal profit.

Example 7

ABC Corporation just purchased a small company that specializes in the manufacture of part No. 510. ABC is a decentralized organization, and will treat the newly acquired company as an autonomous division called Division B with full profit responsibility. Division B's fixed costs total $30,000 per month, and variable costs per unit are $18.

Division B has operating capacity of 5,000 units, which is sufficient to sell as many as 2,500 units to other divisions. The normal selling price per unit is $30.

Division A of ABC Corporation is currently purchasing 2,500 units of part No. 510 per month from an outside supplier at $29 per unit, which represents the normal selling market price $30 price less a quantity discount. Top management is hoping that Division A will consider buying part No. 510 from Division B.

Top management of the company wishes to decide what transfer price should be used. Top management may consider the following alternative prices:

(a) $30 market price

(b) $29, the price that Division A is currently paying to the outside supplier

(c) $23.50 negotiated price, which is $18 variable cost plus 1/2 of the benefits of an internal transfer [($29-$18) x 1/2]

(d) $24 full cost, which is $18 variable cost plus $6 ($30,000/5,000 units) fixed cost per unit

(e) $18 variable cost

We will discuss each of these prices:

(a) $30 would not be an appropriate transfer price. Division B cannot charge a price more than the price Division A is paying now ($29).

(b) $29 would be an appropriate transfer price if top management wishes to treat the divisions as autonomous investment centers. This price would cause all of the benefits of internal transfers to accrue to the selling division, with the buying division's position remaining unchanged.

(c) $23.50 would be an appropriate transfer price if top management wishes to treat the divisions as investment centers, but wishes to share the benefits of an internal transfer equally between them, as follows:

Variable costs of Division B	$18.00
1/2 of the difference between the variable costs of Division B and the price Division A is paying ($29 - $18) x 1/2	5.50
Transfer price	$23.50

Note: $23.50 is just one example of a negotiated transfer price. The exact price depends on how the benefits are divided.

(d) $24 [$24 = $18 + ($30,000 / 5,000 units)] would be an appropriate transfer price if top management treats divisions like cost centers with no profit responsibility. All benefits from both divisions will accrue to the buying division. This will maximize the profits of the company as a whole, but affect adversely the performance of the selling division. Another disadvantage of this cost-based approach is that inefficiencies (if any) of the selling division are being passed on to the buying division.

(e) $18 would be an appropriate transfer price for guiding top management in deciding whether transfers between the two divisions should take place. Since $18 is less than the outside purchase price of the buying division, and the selling division has excess capacity, the transfer should take place, because it will maximize the profits of the company as a whole. However, if $18 is used as a transfer price, then all of the benefits of the internal transfer accrue to the buying division and it will hurt the performance of the selling division.

Chapter Summary

Return on investment (ROI) and residual income (RI) are the two most widely used measures of divisional performance. Emphasis was placed on the breakdown of the ROI formula, commonly referred to as the Du Pont formula. The breakdown formula has several advantages over the original formula in terms of profit planning. The choice of evaluation systems—ROI or RI—will greatly affect a division's investment decisions.

Transfer pricing relates to the price to be charged in an exchange of goods and services between two investment centers within an organization. Unfortunately, there is no single transfer price that is satisfactory to the parties involved in the transfer—the selling division buying division, and top management.

In practical terms, the best transfer price to use is the negotiated market price. However, when that is not available, say for example there is a new product, budgeted cost plus profit markup should be used. In any event, the buying division should never be charged a transfer price that exceeds the outside market price. Whether the buying division is allowed to buy outside or stay inside depends on what is best for corporate profitability.

Chapter 10

Relevant Costs and Short-term Decisions

When performing the manufacturing and selling functions, management is constantly faced with the problem of choosing between alternative courses of action. Typical questions to be answered include: What to make? How to make it? Where to sell the product? and What price should be charged? In the short run, management is faced with many short-term, nonroutine decisions. In a short-term situation, fixed costs are generally irrelevant to the decision at hand. Managerial accountants must recognize as a major decision tool, the two important concepts: relevant costs and contribution margin.

Relevant Costs Defined

In each of the above situations, the ultimate management decision rests on cost data analysis. Cost data are important in many decisions, since they are the basis for profit calculations. Cost data are classified by function, behavior patterns and other criteria, as discussed previously.

However, not all costs are of equal importance in decision making and managers must identify the costs that are relevant to a decision. The relevant costs are the expected future costs (and also revenues) which differ between the decision alternatives. Therefore, the sunk costs (past and historical costs) are not considered relevant in the decision at hand. What are relevant are the incremental or differential costs.

Under the concept of relevant costs, which may be appropriately titled the incremental, differential, or relevant cost approach, the decision involves the following steps:

1. Gather all costs associated with each alternative.
2. Drop the sunk costs.

3. Drop those costs which do not differ between alternatives.
4. Select the best alternative based on the remaining cost data.

Example 1

To illustrate the irrelevance of sunk costs and the relevance of incremental costs, let us consider a replacement decision problem. A company owns a milling machine that was purchased three years ago for $25,000. Its present book value is $17,500. The company is contemplating replacing this machine with a new one which will cost $50,000 and have a five-year useful life. The new machine will generate the same amount of revenue as the old one but will substantially cut down on variable operating costs. Annual sales and operating costs of the present machine and the proposed replacement are based on normal sales volume of 20,000 units and are estimated as follows:

	Present Machine	New Machine
Sales	$60,000	$60,000
Variable costs	35,000	20,000
Fixed costs:		
Depreciation (straight-line)	2,500	10,000
Insurance, taxes, etc.	4,000	4,000
Net income	$18,500	$ 26,000

At first glance, it appears that the new machine provides an increase in net income of $7,500 per year. The book value of the present machine, however, is a sunk cost and is irrelevant in this decision. Furthermore, sales and fixed costs such as insurance, taxes, etc., also are irrelevant since they do not differ between the two alternatives being considered. Eliminating all the irrelevant costs leaves us with only the incremental costs, as follows.

Savings in variable costs	$15,000
Less: Increase in fixed costs	10,000 *
Net annual cash saving arising from the new machine	$5,000

* exclusive of $2,500 sunk cost

Pricing a Special Order

A company often receives a short-term, special order for its products at lower prices than usual. In normal times, the company may refuse such an order since it will not yield a satisfactory profit. If the company has idle (excess) capacity or times are bad, however, such an order should be accepted if the incremental revenue obtained from it exceeds the incremental costs. The company is better off to receive some revenue, above its incremental costs, than to receive nothing at all. he firm must make sure, however, that the products or services involved are sufficiently different from its regular counterparts to avoid violating federal price discrimination laws.

Such a price, one lower than the regular price, is called a contribution price. This approach to pricing is often called the contribution approach to pricing or the variable pricing model. This approach is most appropriate under the following conditions:

(1) There is idle capacity.

(2) The company is operating in a distress situation.

(3) It is faced with sharp competition or in a competitive bidding situation.

Example 2

Assume that a company with 100,000-unit capacity is currently producing and selling only 90,000 units of product each year at a regular price of $2, indicating that the company has idle capacity. If the variable cost per unit is $1 and the annual fixed cost is $45,000, the income statement looks as follows:

Sales (90,000 units)	$180,000	$2.00
Less: variable cost (90,000 units)	90,000	1.00
Contribution margin	$90,000	$1.00
Less: Fixed cost	45,000	0.50
Net income	$45,000	$0.50

The company has just received an order that calls for 10,000 units @ $1.20, for a total of $12,000. The acceptance of this order will not affect regular sales. The company's president is reluctant to accept the order, however, because the $1.20 price is below the $1.50 factory unit cost ($1.50 = $1.00 + $0.50). Should the company accept the order?

The answer is yes. The company can add to total profits by accepting this special order even though the price offered is below the unit factory cost. At a price of $1.20, the order will contribute $0.20 per unit (CM per unit = $1.20 - $1.00 = $0.20) toward fixed cost, and profit will increase by $2,000 (10,000 units x $0.20).

Using the contribution approach to pricing, the variable cost of $1 will be a better guide than the full unit cost of $1.50. Note that the fixed costs do not change because of the presence of idle capacity.

The same result can be seen as follows:

	Per Unit	Without Special Order (90,000 units)	With Special Order (100,000 units)	Difference
Sales	$2.00	$180,000	$192,000	$12,000
Less: Variable costs	1.00	90,000	100,000	10,000
CM	1.00	$ 90,000	$ 92,000	$ 2,000
Less: Fixed cost	0.50	45,000	45,000	0
Net income	$0.50	$ 45,000	$ 47,000	$ 2,000

Example 3

The marketing manager had decided that for Product A he wants a markup of 30 percent over cost. Particulars concerning a unit of Product A are given as follows:

Direct material	$4,000
Direct labor	10,000
Overhead	2,500
Total cost	$16,500
Markup on cost (30%)	4,950
Selling price	$21,450

Total direct labor for the year equals $1,200,000. Total overhead for the year equals 25 percent of direct labor ($300,000), of which 40 percent is fixed and 60 percent is variable. The customer offers to buy a unit of product A for $18,000. Idle capacity exists.

You should accept the extra order because it provides an increased contribution margin, as indicated below:

Selling price		$18,000
Less: Variable costs		
Direct material	$4,000	
Direct labor	10,000	
Variable overhead ($10,000 x 15%)*	1,500	(15,500)
Contribution margin		$2,500
Less: Fixed overhead		(0)
Net Income		$2,500

* Variable overhead equals 15 percent of direct labor, calculated as follows:

$$\frac{\text{Variable overhead}}{\text{Direct labor}} = \frac{60\% \times \$300{,}000}{\$1{,}200{,}000} = \frac{\$180{,}000}{\$1{,}200{,}000} = 15\%$$

Bid Price

The relevant cost approach can be used to determine the bid price on a contract.

Example 4

Travis Company has received an order for 6,000 units. The management accountant wants to know the minimum bid price that would produce a $14,000 increase in profit. The current income statement follows:

Income Statement		
Sales (30,000 units x $20)		$600,000
Less cost of sales		
Direct material	$60,000	
Direct labor	150,000	
Variable overhead (150,000* 40%)	60,000	
Fixed overhead	80,000	(350,000)
Gross margin		$250,000
Less selling and administrative expenses		
Variable (includes transportation costs of $0. 20 per unit)	15,000	
Fixed	85,000	(100,000)
Net income		$150,000

If the contract is taken, the cost patterns for the extra order will remain the same, with these exceptions:

- Transportation costs will be paid by the customer.
- Special tools costing $6,000 will be required for just this order and will not be reusable.
- Direct labor time for each unit under the order will be 10 percent longer.

The bid price is derived in this manner:

	Current Cost Per Unit	
Selling price	$20	($600,000/30,000)
Direct material	2	($60,000/30,000)
Direct labor	5	($150,000/30,000)
Variable overhead	40% of direct labor cost	($60,000/$150,000)
Variable selling and administrative expense	$0.50	($15,000/30,000)

As can be seen in the income statement on the next page, the contract price for the 6,000 units should be $80,000 ($680,000-$600,000), or $13.33 per unit ($80,000/6,000). The contract price per unit of $13.33 is less than the $20 current selling price per unit. Note that by accepting the order, total fixed cost will remain the same except for the $6,000 cost of special tools.

Income Statement

	30,000 Current	36,000 Projected
Sales	$ 600,000	$680,000 (d) Computed last
Cost of sales		
Direct material	$60,000	$72,000 ($2 x 36,000)
Direct labor	150,000	183,000 ($150,000 + [6,000 x $5.50 (a)])
Variable overhead	$60,000	$73,200 ($183,000 x 40%)
Fixed overhead	80,000	86,000 ($80,000 + $6,000)
Total	$350,000	$414,200
Variable selling and administration costs	$15,000	$16,800 ($15,000 + [6,000 x $0.30]) (b)
Fixed selling and administrative costs	85,000	85,000
Total	$100,000	$101,800
Net income	$150,000	$164,000 (d)

(a) $5 * 1.10 = $5.50

(b) $0.50 - $0.20 = $0.30

(c) $150,000 + $14,000 = $164,000

(d) Net income + selling and administrative expensive + cost of sales = sales

$164,000 + $101,800 + $414,200 = $680,000

Outsourcing: The Make-or-Buy Decision

Often companies purchase subcomponents used to make their products instead of making them in their in-house manufacturing facilities. Buying services, products or components of products from outside vendors instead of producing them is called outsourcing. The decision whether to produce a subcomponent in-house or to buy it externally from an outside vendor is called a make-or-buy (outsource) decision. Examples include:

(1) Payroll processing in-house or outsource it to an outside service bureau;

(2) developing a training program in-house or sending employees outside for training; and

(3) providing data processing and network services internally or buying them.

Other strong candidates for outsourcing include: managing fleets of vehicles, sales and marketing, and custodial services.

This decision involves both quantitative and qualitative factors. The qualitative factors include ensuring product quality and the necessity for long-run business relationships with the supplier. The quantitative factors deal with cost. The quantitative effects of the make-or-buy decision are best seen through the relevant cost approach.

Example 5

Assume that a firm has prepared the following cost estimates for the manufacture of a subassembly component based on an annual production of 8,000 units:

	Per Unit	Total
Direct materials	$5	$40,000
Direct labor	4	32,000
Variable factory overhead applied	4	32,000
Fixed factory overhead applied (150% of direct labor cost)	6	48,000
Total cost	$19	$152,000

The supplier has offered to provide the subassembly at a price of $16 each. Two-thirds of fixed factory overhead, which represents executive salaries, rent, depreciation and taxes, continue regardless of the decision. Should the company buy or make the product?

The key to the decision lies in the investigation of those relevant costs that change between the make-or-buy alternatives. Assuming that the productive capacity will be idle if not used to produce the subassembly, the analysis takes the following form:

	Per Unit		Total of 8,000 Unit	
	Make	Buy	Make	Buy
Purchase price		$16		$128,000
Direct materials	$5		$40,000	
Direct labor	4		32,000	
Variable overhead	4		32,000	
Fixed overhead that can be avoided by not making	2		16,000	
Total relevant costs	$15	$16	$120,000	$128,000
Difference in favor of making	$1		$8,000	

The make-or-buy decision must be investigated, along with the broader perspective of considering how best to utilize available facilities. The alternatives are:

1. Leaving facilities idle;
2. buying the parts and renting out idle facilities; and
3. buying the parts and using idle facilities for other products.

The Sell-or-process-further Decision

When two or more products are produced simultaneously from the same input by a joint process, these products are called joint products. The term joint costs is used to describe all the manufacturing costs incurred prior to the point where the joint products are identified as individual products, referred to as the split-off point. At the split-off point some of the joint products are in final form and saleable to the consumer, whereas others require additional processing.

In many cases, however, the company might have an option: it can sell the goods at the split-off point or process them further in the hope of obtaining additional revenue. In connection with this type of decision, called the sell-or-process-further decision, joint costs are considered irrelevant, since the joint costs have already been incurred at the time of the decision, and therefore represent sunk costs. The decision will rely exclusively on additional revenue compared to the additional costs incurred due to further processing.

Example 6

The Bailey Company produces three products, A, B and C from a joint process. Joint production costs for the year were $120,000. Product A may be sold at the split-off point or processed further. The additional processing requires no special facilities and all additional processing costs are variable. Sales values and cost needed to evaluate the company's production policy regarding product A follow:

		Additional Cost & Sales Value after Further Processing	
Units Produced	Sales Value at Split-Off	Sales	Costs
3,000	$60,000	$90,000	$25,000

Should product A be sold at the split-off point or processed further?

Incremental sales revenue	$30,000
Incremental costs (variable), additional processing	25,000
Incremental gain (CM)	$5,000

In summary, product A should be processed as shown above. Keep in mind that the joint production cost of $120,000 is not included in the analysis, since it is a sunk cost and, therefore, irrelevant to the decision.

Keeping or Dropping A Product Line

Another type of nonrecurring decisions managers must face is whether to keep or drop unprofitable segments, such as product lines, services, sales territories, divisions or departments. The goal of this decision analysis, known as segment profitability analysis, is to identify the segments that have a negative segment margin. A segment margin is a segment's sales revenue minus its direct costs (variables costs and direct fixed costs identified with the segment).

The decision whether to drop an old product line or add a new one must take into account both qualitative and quantitative factors. However, any final decision should be based primarily on the impact the decision will have on the company's overall contribution margin or net income.

Example 7

Alpha-Omega Grocery Store has three major product lines: produce, meats and canned food. The store is considering the decision to drop the meat line because the income statement shows it is being sold at a loss. Note the income statement for these product lines below:

		Canned Produce	Meats	Food	Total
Sales		$10,000	$15,000	$25,000	$50,000
Less:	Variable Costs	6,000	8,000	12,000	26,000
CM		$4,000	7,000	13,000	$24,000
Less:	Fixed costs				
	Direct	$2,000	$6,500	$4,000	$12,500
	Allocated	1,000	1,500	2,500	5,000
Total		$3,000	$8,000	$6,500	$17,500
Net income		$1,000	$(1,000)	$6,500	$6,500

In this example, direct fixed costs are those costs that are identified directly with each of the product lines, whereas allocated fixed costs are the amount of common fixed costs allocated to the product lines using some base such as space occupied. The amount of common fixed costs typically continues regardless of the decision and thus cannot be saved by dropping the product line to which it is distributed.

The comparative approach showing the effects on the company as a whole with and without the meat line is shown below:

		Keep Meats	Drop Meats	Difference
Sales		$50,000	$35,000	$(15,000)
Less:	Variable cost	26,000	18,000	(8,000)
CM		$24,000	$17,000	$(7,000)
Less:	Fixed cost			
	Direct	$12,500	$6,000	$(6,500)
	Allocated	5,000	5,000	0
	Total	$17,500	$11,000	$(6,500)
Net income		$6,500	$6,000	$(500)

Alternatively, the incremental approach would show the following:

If Meats Dropped	
CM lost	$7,000
Gains: Direct fixed costs avoided	6,500
Increase (decrease) in net income	$(500)

From either of the two methods, we see that by dropping meats the store will lose an additional $500. Therefore, the meat product line should be kept. One of the great dangers in allocating common fixed costs is that such allocations can make a product line look less profitable than it really is. Because of such an allocation, the meat line showed a loss of $1,000, but it in effect contributes $500 ($7,000 - $6,500) to the recovery of the store's common fixed costs.

Product Mix Decisions in the Presence of Limited Resources

In general, the emphasis on products with higher contribution margin maximizes a firm's total net income, even though total sales may decrease. This is not true, however, where there are constraining factors and scarce resources. The constraining factor may be machine hours, labor hours or cubic feet of warehouse space.

In the presence of these constraining factors, maximizing total profits depends on getting the highest contribution margin per unit of the factor (rather than the highest contribution margin per unit of product output).

Example 8

Assume that a company produces two products, A and B, with the following contribution margins per unit.

	A	B
Sales	$8	$24
Variable costs	6	20
CM	$2	$4
Annual fixed costs	$42,000	

As is indicated by CM per unit, B is more profitable than A since it contributes more to the company's total profits than A ($4 vs. $2). But let us assume that the firm has a limited capacity of 10,000 labor hours. Further, assume that A requires two labor hours to produce and B requires five labor hours. One way to express this limited capacity is to determine the contribution margin per labor hour.

	A	B
CM/unit	$2.00	$4.00
Labor hours required per unit	2	5
CM per labor hour	$1.00	$0.80

Since A returns the higher CM per labor hour, it should be produced and B should be dropped. Another way to look at the problem is to calculate total CM for each product.

	A	B
Maximum possible production	5,000 units*	2,000 units**
CM per unit	$2	$4
Total CM	$10,000	$8,000

* (10,000 hours / 2 hours)

**(10,000 hours / 5 hours)

Again, product A should be produced since it contributes more than B ($10,000 vs. $8,000).

Note: The presence of only one limited resource is unrealistic. Virtually all firms encounter multiple constraints: restrictions on materials, labor inputs, demand for each product, warehouse space, display space and so on. The solution of the product mix problem with multiple constraints is considerably more complex and requires a technique known as linear programming.

Theory of Constraints

A binding constraint can limit a company's profitability. For example, a manufacturing company may have a bottleneck operation, through which every unit of a product must pass before moving on to other operations. The theory of constraints (TOC) calls for identifying such limiting constraints and seeking ways to relax them. Also referred to as managing constraints, this management approach can significantly improve an organization's level of goal attainment. Among the ways that management can relax a constraint by expanding the capacity of a bottleneck operation are the following:

- Outsource (subcontracting) all or part of the bottle neck operation.
- Invest in additional production equipment and employing parallel processing, in which multiple product units undergo the same production operation simultaneously.
- Work overtime at the bottleneck operation.
- Retrain employees and shifting them to the bottleneck.
- Eliminate any non-value-added activities at the bottleneck operation.

You should remember

Identification of the relevant costs and benefits is an important step in making any economic decision. Nonetheless, one often overlooks relevant costs or incorrectly includes irrelevant data. Keep in mind four common mistakes to avoid in decision making.

1. Sunk costs. The book value of an asset, defined as its acquisition cost less the accumulated depreciation, is a sunk cost. Sunk costs cannot be changed by any current or future course of action, so they are irrelevant in decision making. Nevertheless, a common behavioral tendency is to give undue importance to book values in decisions that involve replacing an asset or disposing of obsolete inventory. Managers often seek to justify their past decisions by refusing to dispose of an asset, if a better alternative has been identified. Ignore sunk costs.
2. Unitized fixed costs. For product-costing purposes, fixed costs are unitized (divided by some activity measure) and assigned to individual units of product. The result is to make fixed cost appear variable. While there are legitimate reasons for this practice, from a product-costing perspective, it can create confusion in decision making. Therefore, in a decision analysis it is usually wise to include a fixed cost in its total amount, rather than as a per-unit cost. Beware of unitized fixed costs in decision making.
3. Allocated fixed costs. It is also common to allocate fixed costs across divisions, departments or product lines. A possible result is that a product or department may appear unprofitable when in reality it does make a

contribution toward covering fixed costs and profit. Before deciding to eliminate a department, be sure to ask which costs will be avoided if a particular alternative is selected. Beware of allocated fixed costs; identify the avoidable costs.

4. Opportunity costs. Managers tend to overlook opportunity costs, or to treat such costs as less important than out-of-pocket costs. Yet opportunity costs are just as real and important to making a correct decision, as are out-of-pocket costs. Pay special attention to identifying and including opportunity costs in a decision analysis.

Chapter Summary

Not all costs are of equal importance in decision making and managerial accountants must identify those costs that are relevant to a decision. The relevant costs are the expected future costs that differ between the decision alternatives. Therefore, the sunk costs are irrelevant since they are past and historical costs. The costs that continue regardless of the decision are irrelevant.

What are relevant are the incremental or differential costs. The relevant cost approach assists managerial accountants in making short-term, nonroutine decisions such as whether to accept a below-normal selling price, which products to emphasize, whether to make or buy, whether to sell or process further, how to formulate a bid price on a contract and how to optimize utilization of capacity. Table 10.1 summarizes guidelines for typical short-tern decisions.

Table 10.1: Decision Guidelines

Decision	Description	Decision Guidelines
Special order	Should a discount-priced order be accepted when there is idle capacity?	If regular orders are not affected, accept order exceeds the incremental cost. Fixed costs are usually irrelevant.
Make or buy	Should a part be made or bought by a vendor?	Choose lower- cost option. Fixed costs are usually irrelevant. Often opportunity costs are present.
Closing a segment	Should a segment be dropped?	Compare loss in contribution margin with saving in fixed costs.

Decision	Description	Decision Guidelines
Sell or process further	Should joint products be sold at split- off or processed further?	Ignore joint costs. Process further if incremental revenue exceeds incremental cost.
Scarce resources	Which products should be emphasized with limited resource?	Emphasize products with highest contribution margin. per unit of scarce resource (e.g., CM per machine hour).

Chapter 11

Long-term Investment and Capital Budgeting Decisions

Capital budgeting is the process of making long-term planning decisions for alternative investment opportunities. There are many investment decisions that the company may have to make in order to grow. Examples of capital budgeting applications are product line selection, keep or sell a business segment, lease or buy and which asset to invest in.

What Are the Types of Investment Projects?

There are typically two types of long-term investment decisions:

1. Selection decisions in terms of obtaining new facilities or expanding existing ones: Examples include:
   (a) Investments in property, plant and equipment as well as other types of assets;
   (b) resource commitments in the form of new product development, market research, introduction of a computer, refunding of long-term debt and so on; and
   (c) mergers and acquisitions in the form of buying another company to add a new product line.
2. Replacement decisions in terms of replacing existing facilities with new ones. Examples include replacing an old machine with a high-tech machine.

What Are the Features of Investment Projects?

Long-term investments have three important features:

First, they typically involve a large amount of initial cash outlays which tend to have a long-term impact on the firm's future profitability. Therefore, this initial cash outlay needs to be justified on a cost-benefit basis. Second, there are expected recurring cash inflows (for example, increased revenues, savings in cash operating expenses, etc.) over the life of the investment project. This frequently requires considering the time value of money. And, income taxes could make a difference in the accept or reject decision. Therefore, income tax factors must be taken into account in every capital budgeting decision.

Understanding the Concept of Time Value of Money

The time value of money, a measure of financial opportunity costs, is the cost of money that is borrowed or lent. It is based on the fact that a dollar received today is worth more than a dollar to be received one year from today. This statement sums up an important principle: money has a time value. The truth of this principle is not that inflation might make the dollar received at a later time worth less in buying power. The reason is that you could invest the dollar now and have more than a dollar at the specified later date.

Time value of money is a critical consideration in financial and investment decisions. It has two major components: future value and present value. Future value, which may be referred to as compounding is future sums of money resulting from an investment. Present value, which is calculated through a process called discounting, is inversely related to compounding and used to evaluate the future cash flow associated with capital budgeting projects. There are numerous applications of the time value of money in accounting and finance.

How Do You Calculate Future Values – How Money Grows?

A dollar in hand today is worth more than a dollar to be received tomorrow because of the interest it could earn from putting it in a savings account or placing it in an investment account. Compounding interest means that interest earns interest. For the discussion of the concepts of compounding and time value, let us define:

F_n = future value: the amount of money at the end of year n

P = principal

i = annual interest rate

n = number of years

Then:

F_1 = the amount of money at the end of year 1

= principal and interest = $P + iP = P(1+i)$

F_2 = the amount of money at the end of year 2

$= F_1(1+i) = P(1+i)(1+i) = P(1+i)^2$

The future value of an investment compounded annually at rate i for n years is

$$F_n = P \bullet (1+i)^n = P \bullet T1(i,n)$$

where T1(i,n) is the compound amount of $1 and can be found in Table 1 in the Appendix.

Example 1

You place $1,000 in a savings account earning 8 percent interest compounded annually. How much money will you have in the account at the end of 4 years?

$$F_n = P(1+i)^n$$

$$F_4 = \$1,000\ (1 + 0.08)^4 = \$1,000\ T1(8\%,4 \text{ years})$$

From Table 1, the T1 for 4 years at 8 percent is 1.361.

Therefore: $F_4 = \$1,000\ (1.361) = \$1,361$.

Example 2

You invested a large sum of money in the stock of Delta Corporation. The company paid a $3 dividend per share. The dividend is expected to increase by 20 percent per year for the next 3 years. You wish to project the dividends for years 1 through 3.

$$F_n = P(1+i)^n$$

$$F_1 = \$3(1+0.2)^1 = \$3\ T1(20\%,1) = \$3\ (1.200) = \$3.60$$

$$F_2 = \$3(1+0.2)^2 = \$3\ T1(20\%,2) = \$3\ (1.440) = \$4.32$$

$$F_3 = \$3(1+0.2)^3 = \$3\ T1(20\%,3) = \$3\ (1.728) = \$5.18$$

Future Value of an Annuity

An annuity is defined as a series of payments (or receipts) of a fixed amount for a specified number of periods. Each payment is assumed to occur at the end of the period. The future value of an annuity is a compound annuity which involves depositing or investing an equal sum of money at the end of each year for a certain number of years and allowing it to grow.

Let S_n = the future value on an n-year annuity

A = the amount of an annuity

Then we can write:

$$S_n = A(1+i)^{n-1} + A(1+i)^{n-2} + \dots + A(1+i)^0$$
$$= A[(1+i)^{n-1}+(1+i)^{n-2}+ \dots + (1+i)^0]$$
$$S_n = A \bullet \sum_{t=0}^{n-1}(1+i)^t = A \bullet \left(\frac{(1+i)^n}{i}\right) = A \bullet T2(i, n)$$

where T2(i,n) represents the future value of an annuity of $1 for n years compounded at i percent and can be found in Table 2 in the Appendix.

Example 3

You wish to determine the sum of money you will have in a savings account at the end of 6 years by depositing $1,000 at the end of each year for the next 6 years. The annual interest rate is 8 percent. The T2(8%,6 years) is given in Table 2 as 7.336. Therefore:

$$S_6 = \$1{,}000\ T2(8\%,6) = \$1{,}000\ (7.336) = \$7{,}336$$

Example 4

You deposit $30,000 semiannually into a fund for ten years. The annual interest rate is 8 percent. The amount accumulated at the end of the tenth year is calculated as follows:

$$S_n = A.\ T2(i, n)$$

where A = $30,000

$i = 8\%/2 = 4\%$

$n = 10 \times 2 = 20$

Therefore:

$$S_n = \$30{,}000\ T2(4\%, 20)$$
$$= \$30{,}000\ (29.778) = \$893{,}340$$

What Is Present Value – How Much Money Is Worth Now?

Present value is the present worth of future sums of money. The process of calculating present values, or discounting, is actually the opposite of finding the compounded future value. In connection with present value calculations, the interest rate i is called the discount rate. The discount rate we use is more commonly called the cost of capital, which is the minimum rate of return required by the investor.

Recall that $F_n = P(1+i)^n$

Therefore:

$$P = \frac{F_n}{(1+i)^n} = F_n \bullet \left(\frac{1}{(1+i)^n}\right) = F_n \bullet T3(i, n)$$

Where T3(i,n) represents the present value of $1 and is given in Table 3 in the Appendix.

Example 5

You have been given an opportunity to receive $20,000 6 years from now. If you can earn 10 percent on your investments, what is the most you should pay for this opportunity? To answer this question, you must compute the present value of $20,000 to be received 6 years from now at a 10 percent rate of discount. F_6 is $20,000, I is 10 percent, and n is 6 years. T3(10%,6) from Table 3 is 0.565.

$$P = \$20{,}000\left(\frac{1}{(1+0.1)^6}\right) = \$20{,}000\ T3(10\%,6) = \$20{,}000(0.564) = \$11{,}280$$

This means that you can earn 10 percent on your investment, and you would be indifferent to receiving $11,280 now or $20,000 6 years from today since the amounts are time equivalent. In other words, you could invest $11,300 today at 10 percent and have $20,000 in 6 years.

Present Value of Mixed Streams of Cash Flows

The present value of a series of mixed payments (or receipts) is the sum of the present value of each individual payment. We know that the present value of each individual payment is the payment times the appropriate T3 value.

Example 6

You are thinking of starting a new product line that initially costs $32,000. Your annual projected cash inflows are:

1 $10,000

2 $20,000

3 $5,000

If you must earn a minimum of 10 percent on your investment, should you undertake this new product line? The present value of this series of mixed streams of cash inflows is calculated as follows:

Year	Cash inflows	x T3(10%, n)	Present Value
1	$10,000	0.909	$9,090
2	$20,000	0.826	$16,520
3	$5,000	0.751	$3,755
			$29,365

Since the present value of your projected cash inflows is less than the initial investment, you should not undertake this project.

Present Value of an Annuity

Interest received from bonds, pension funds, and insurance obligations all involve annuities. To compare these financial instruments, we need to know the present value of each. The present value of an annuity (P_n) can be found by using the following equation:

$$P_n = A \bullet \frac{1}{(1+i)^1} + A \bullet \frac{1}{(1+i)^2} + \ldots + A \bullet \frac{1}{(1+i)^n}$$

$$= A \bullet \left[\frac{1}{(1+i)^1} + \frac{1}{(1+i)^2} + \ldots + \frac{1}{(1+i)^n} \right]$$

$$P_n = A \bullet \sum_{t=0}^{n} \frac{1}{(1+i)^t} = A \bullet \left[\frac{1}{i}\left(1 - \frac{1}{(1+i)}\right) \right] = A \bullet T4(i,n)$$

where T4(i,n) represents the present value of an annuity of $1 discounted at i percent for n years and is found in Table 4 in the Appendix.

Example 7

Assume that the cash inflows in Example 6 form an annuity of $10,000 for 3 years. Then the present value is:

$$P_n = A \cdot T4(i,n)$$
$$P_3 = \$10,000\ T4(10\%, 3\ years) = \$10,000\ (2.487) = \$24,870$$

Use of Financial Calculators and Spreadsheet Programs

There are many financial calculators that contain pre-programmed formulas to perform many present value and future applications. They include Hewlett-Packard 10B, Sharpe EL733 and Texas Instrument BA35. Furthermore, spreadsheet software such as Excel has built-in financial functions to perform many such applications.

How Do You Measure Investment Worth?

Several methods of evaluating investment projects are as follows:

1. payback period
2. accounting rate of return (ARR)
3. internal rate of return (IRR)
4. net present value (NPV)
5. profitability index (or present value index)

The NPV method and the IRR method are called discounted cash flow (DCF) methods. Each of these methods is discussed below.

Payback Period

The payback period measures the length of time required to recover the amount of initial investment. It is computed by dividing the initial investment by the cash inflows through increased revenues or cost savings.

$$\text{Payback period} = \frac{\text{Initial Investment}}{\text{Annual Cash Inflows}}$$

Example 8

Assume:

Cost of investment	$18,000
Annual cash savings	$3,000

Then, the payback period is:

$$\text{Payback period} = \frac{\text{Initial investment}}{\text{Cost savings}} = \frac{\$18{,}000}{\$3{,}000} = 6 \text{ years}$$

Decision rule: Choose the project with the shorter payback period. The rationale behind this choice is: The shorter the payback period, the less risky the project, and the greater the liquidity.

Example 9

Consider the two projects whose after-tax cash inflows are not even. Assume each project costs $1,000.

	Cash Inflow	
Year	A($)	B($)
1	100	500
2	200	400
3	300	300
4	400	100
5	500	
6	600	

When cash inflows are not even, the payback period has to be found by trial and error. The payback period of project A is 4 years ($1,000= $100 + $200 + $300 + $400). The payback period of project B is 2 1/3 years ($1,000 = $500 + $400 + $100):

$$2 \text{ years} + \frac{\$100}{\$300} = 2\ 1/3 \text{ years}$$

Project B is the project of choice in this case, since it has the shorter payback period.

The advantages of using the payback period method of evaluating an investment project are that it is simple to compute and easy to understand and it handles investment risk effectively. The shortcomings of this method are that it does not recognize the time value of money and it ignores the impact of cash inflows received after the payback period; essentially, cash flows after the payback period determine profitability of an investment.

Accounting Rate of Return

Accounting rate of return (ARR), also called simple or unadjusted rate of return, measures profitability from the conventional accounting standpoint by relating the required initial investment (I)—or sometimes the average investment—to the future average annual income.

$$\text{ARR} = \frac{\text{Project's Average Annual Income}}{\text{Initial (or Average) Investment}}$$

Average investment is defined as follows:

$$\text{Average investment} = \frac{(I - S)}{2} + S$$

$$\text{or simply } \frac{I}{2} \quad \text{if } S = 0$$

where I = initial (original) investment and S = salvage value.

Decision rule: Under the ARR method, choose the project with the higher rate of return.

Example 10

Consider the following investment:

Initial investment (I)	\$6,500
Estimated life	20 years
Cash inflows per year	\$1,000
Depreciation per year (using straight line)	\$325
Salvage value (S)	0

The accounting rate of return for this project is:

$$\text{ARR} = \frac{\text{Average income}}{\text{Investment}} = \frac{\$1,000 - \$325}{\$6,500} = 10.4\%$$

If average investment is used, then:

$$\text{ARR} = \frac{\$1,000 - \$325}{\$6,500/2} = \frac{\$675}{\$3,250} = 20.8\%$$

The advantages of this method are that it is easily understood, simple to compute and recognizes the profitability factor. The shortcomings of this method are that it fails to recognize the time value of money, and it uses accounting data instead of cash flow data.

Internal Rate of Return

Internal rate of return (IRR), also called time adjusted rate of return, Is defined as the rate of interest that equates I with the PV of future cash inflows.

In other words:

at IRR, I = PV

(or NPV = 0

Decision rule: Accept the project if the IRR exceeds the cost of capital. Otherwise, reject it.

Example 11

Consider the following investment:

Initial investment	\$12,950
Estimated life	10 years
Annual cash inflows	\$3,000
Cost of capital (minimum required rate of return)	12%

We set the following equality (I = PV):

$$\$12{,}950 = \$3{,}000 \cdot T4(i, 10 \text{ years})$$

$$T4(i, 10 \text{ years}) = \frac{\$12{,}950}{\$3{,}000} = 4.317$$

which stands somewhere between 18 percent and 20 percent in the 10-year line of Table 4. The interpolation follows:

	PV of An Annuity of $1 Factor T4(i,10 years)	
18%	4.494	4.494
IRR	4.317	
20%		4.192
Difference	0.177	0.302

Therefore,

$$IRR = 18\% + \frac{0.177}{0.302} (20\% - 18\%)$$

$$= 18\% + 0.586(2\%) = 18\% + 1.17\% = 19.17\%$$

Since the IRR of the investment is greater than the cost of capital (12 percent), accept the project.

The advantage of using the IRR method is that it does consider the time value of money and, therefore, is more exact and realistic than the ARR method. The shortcomings of this method are that it is time-consuming to compute, especially when the cash inflows are not even, although most financial calculators and PCs have a key to calculate IRR, and it fails to recognize the varying sizes of investment in competing projects.

Net Present Value

Net present value (NPV) is the difference between the present value (PV) of the cash inflows and the initial investment (I) associated with a project:

$$NPV = PV - I$$

The present value of future cash flows is computed using the so-called cost of capital (or minimum required rate of return) as the discount rate. When cash inflows are uniform, the present value would be:

$$PV = A \,.\, T4\ (i, n)$$

where A is the amount of the annuity. The value of T4 is found in Table 4 of the Appendix.

Decision rule: If NPV is positive, accept the project. Otherwise reject it.

Example 12

Assume the same data given in Example 11, and the net present value of the cash inflows is:

PV	$= A \cdot T4(i,n)$	
	$= \$3{,}000 \cdot T4(12\%, 10 \text{ years})$	
	$= \$3{,}000\ (5.650)$	\$16,950
Initial investment (I)		12,950
Net present value (NPV = PV - I)		\$4,000

Since the NPV of the investment is positive, the investment should be accepted.

The advantages of the NPV method are that it obviously recognizes the time value of money and it is easy to compute whether the cash flows form an annuity or vary from period to period.

Can a Computer Help?

Spreadsheet programs can be used in making IRR calculations. For example, Excel has a function IRR(values, guess). Excel considers negative numbers as cash outflows such as the initial investment, and positive numbers as cash inflows. Many financial calculators have similar features. As in Example 13, suppose you want to calculate the IRR of a \$12,950 investment (the value --12950 entered in year 0 that is followed by 10 monthly cash inflows of 3,000). Using a guess of 12% (the value of 0.12), which is in effect the cost of capital, your formula would be @IRR(values, 0.12) and Excel would return 19.15%, as shown below.

Year 0	1	2	3	4	5	6	7	8	9	10
(12,950)	3,000	3,000	3,000	3,000	3,000	3,000	3,000	3,000	3,000	3,000

IRR = 19.15%

NPV = \$4,000.67

Note: The Excel formula for NPV is NPV (discount rate, cash inflow values) + I, where I is given as a negative number.

> **You should remember**
>
> **Summary of Decision Rules Using Both IRR and NPV Methods**
>
> Internal Rate of Return (IRR)
>
> - Using the present-value tables (T3 or T4), financial calculator, or Excel, computer the IRR.
> - If the IRR exceeds the cost of capital, accept the project; if not, reject the project.
>
> Net Present Value (NPV)
>
> - Calculate the NPV, using the cost of capital as the discount rate.
> - If the NPV is positive, accept the project; otherwise, reject the project.

Profitability Index

The profitability index, also called present value index, is the ratio of the total PV of future cash inflows to the initial investment, that is:

$$\text{Profitability Index} = \frac{PV}{I}$$

This index is used as a means of ranking projects in descending order of attractiveness. Decision rule: If the profitability index is greater than 1, then accept the project.

Example 13

Using the data in Example 11, the profitability index is:

$$\frac{PV}{I} = \frac{\$16,950}{\$12,950} = 1.31$$

Since this project generates $1.31 for each dollar invested (i.e., its profitability index is greater than 1), accept the project. The profitability index has the advantage of putting all projects on the same relative basis regardless of size.

How to Select the Best Mix of Projects with a Limited Budget

Many firms specify a limit on the overall budget for capital spending. Capital rationing is concerned with the problem of selecting the mix of acceptable projects that provides the highest overall NPV. The profitability index is used widely in ranking projects competing for limited funds.

Example 14

The Westmont Company has a fixed budget of $250,000. It needs to select a mix of acceptable projects from the following:

Projects	I($)	PV($)	NPV($)	Profitability Index	Ranking
A	70,000	112,000	42,000	1.60	1
B	100,000	145,000	45,000	1.45	2
C	110,000	126,500	16,500	1.15	5
D	60,000	79,000	19,000	1.32	3
E	40,000	38,000	-2,000	0.95	6
F	80,000	95,000	15,000	1.19	4

The ranking resulting from the profitability index shows that the company should select projects A, B, and D.

	I	PV
A	$70,000	$112,000
B	100,000	145,000
D	60,000	79,000
	$230,000	$336,000

Therefore:

NPV = $336,000 - $230,000 = $106,000

Chapter Summary

We have examined the process of evaluating investment projects. We have also discussed five commonly used criteria for evaluating capital budgeting projects, including the net present value (NPV) and internal rate of return (IRR) methods. The problems that arise with capital rationing were addressed. Throughout this chapter, we assumed no income taxes.

Chapter 12

A Further Look at Capital Budgeting

Income taxes make a difference in many capital budgeting decisions. In other words, the project which is attractive on a before-tax basis may have to be rejected on an after-tax basis. Income taxes typically affect both the amount and the timing of cash flows. Since net income, not cash inflows, is subject to tax, after-tax cash inflows are not usually the same as after-tax net income.

How Do Income Taxes Affect Investment Decisions?

We will show how to calculate after-tax cash flows.

Let us define:

S = Sales

E = Cash operating expenses

d = Depreciation

t = Tax rate

Note: Before-tax cash inflows (or cash savings) = S - E and

Net income = S - E - d

By definition:

After-tax cash inflows = Before-tax cash inflows – Taxes

= (S - E) - (S - E - d) (t)

Rearranging gives the short-cut formula:

After-tax cash inflows	$= (S - E)(1 - t)$	$+ (d)(t)$
	= After-tax cash inflow from operations	+ Tax shield
or		
	= After tax net income	+ depreciation
	$= (S - E - d)(1 - t)$	$+ d$

As can be seen, the deductibility of depreciation from sales in arriving at taxable net income reduces income tax payments and thus serves as a tax shield.

Tax shield = Tax savings on depreciation = (d)(t)

Example 1:

Assume:

$S = \$12,000$

$E = \$10,000$

$d = \$500$ per year using the straight line method

$t = 30\%$

Then:

After-tax cash inflow = (\$12,000 - \$10,000) (1 - .3) + (\$500)(.3)
= (\$2,000)(.7) + (\$500)(.3)
= \$1,400 + \$150 = \$1,550

Note that a tax shield = tax savings on depreciation = (d)(t)
= (\$500)(.3) = \$150

Since the tax shield is dt, the higher the depreciation deduction, the higher the tax savings on depreciation. Therefore, an accelerated depreciation method (such as double-declining balance) produces higher tax savings than the straight-line method. Accelerated methods produce higher present values for the tax savings which may make a given investment more attractive.

Example 2

The Navistar Company estimates that it can save \$2,500 a year in cash operating costs for the next ten years if it buys a special-purpose machine at a cost of \$10,000. No residual value is expected. Depreciation is by straight-line. Assume that the income tax rate is 30 percent, and the after-tax cost of capital (minimum required rate of return) is 10 percent. Should the company buy the machine? Use the NPV method.

Step 1: Calculate after-tax cash savings:

Note that depreciation by straight-line is $10,000/10 = $1,000 per year. Thus:

After-tax cash savings = (S - E) (1 - t) + (d)(t)
= $2,500(1 - .3) + $1,000(.3)
= $1,750 + $300 = $2,050

Step 2: To see if this machine should be purchased, the net present value can be calculated.

PV = $2,050 T4(10%, 10 years) = $2,050 (6.145)=$12,597.25

Thus, NPV = PV - I = $12,597.25 - $10,000 = $2,597.25

Since NPV is positive, the machine should be bought.

Example 3

The CFO of a small appliance maker estimates the sales revenue, cash operating expenses and cash inflows before taxes shown in columns 1, 2 and 3 of the table below, if it buys a high tech machine at a cost of $1,000,000. No residual value is expected. Life is 5 years. Depreciation is by straight-line. Assume that the income tax rate is 35 percent, and the after-tax cost of capital (minimum required rate of return) is percent. Should the company buy the machine? Use the NPV method.

The process of arriving at net cash flow after taxes are shown in columns 4, 5, 6, 7 and 8.

Year	Sales (S) (1)	Cash Operating Expenses (E) (2)	Cash Inflow Before Taxes (S-E) (3)=(1)-(2)	Depreciation (noncash Expense) (d) (4) = 1,000,000/5	Net Income Before Taxes (5) = (3) - (4)	Income Taxes (6) = .35 x (5)	Net Income After Taxes (7)=(5)-(6)	Cash Inflow After Taxes (8)=(3)-(6) or (7)+(4)
1	$1,000,000	$625,000	$375,000	$200,000	$175,000	$61,250	$113,750	$313,750
2	$900,000	$610,000	$290,000	$200,000	$90,000	$31,500	$58,500	$258,500
3	$925,000	$635,000	$290,000	$200,000	$90,000	$31,500	$58,500	$258,500
4	$930,000	$605,000	$325,000	$200,000	$125,000	$43,750	$81,250	$281,250
5	$825,000	$557,000	$268,000	$200,000	$68,000	$23,800	$44,200	$244,200

The NPV of the machine can be calculated using Table 3, as shown below.

Year	Cash Inflow After Taxes	T3 at 10% Table value	PV
1	$ 313,750	0.909	$ 285,199
2	$ 258,500	0.826	$ 213,521
3	$ 258,500	0.751	$ 194,134
4	$ 281,250	0.683	$ 192,094
5	$ 244,200	0.621	$ 151,648
			$ 1,036,596

Thus, NPV = PV - I = $1,036,596 - $1,000,000 = $36,596. Since NPV is positive, the machine should be bought.

Example 4

Shalimar Corporation has provided its revenues and cash operating costs (excluding depreciation) for the old and the new machine, as follows:

	Revenue	Annual Cash Operating Costs	Net Profit before Depreciation and Taxes
Old machine	$150,000	$70,000	$80,000
New machine	$180,000	$60,000	$120,000

Assume that the annual depreciation of the old machine and the new machine will be $30,000 and $50,000, respectively. Assume further that the tax rate is 46 percent. To arrive at net profit after taxes, we first have to deduct depreciation expense from the net profit before depreciation and taxes, as follows:

	Net Profits after Taxes	Add Depreciation	After-Tax Cash Inflows
Old machine	($80,000-$30,000)(1-0.46)=$27,000	$30,000	$57,000
New machine	($120,000-$50,000)(1-0.46)=$37,800	$50,000	$87,800

Subtracting the after-tax cash inflows of the old machine from the cash inflows of the new machine results in the relevant, or incremental, cash inflows for each year. Therefore, in this example, the relevant or incremental cash inflows for each year are $87,800 - $57,000 = $30,800.

Alternatively, the incremental cash inflows after taxes can be computed, using the following simple formula:

After-tax incremental cash inflows = (increase in revenues)(1-tax rate)
– (increase in cash charges)(1-tax rate)
+ (increase in depreciation expenses)(tax rate)

Example 5

Using the data in Example 4, after-tax incremental cash inflows for each year are:

Increase in revenue x (1-tax rate):	
($180,000-$150,000)(1-0.46)	$16,200
– Increase in cash charges x (1-tax rate):	
($60,000-$70,000)(1-0.46)	-(-5,400)
+ Increase in depreciation expense x	
tax rate: ($50,000-$30,000)(0.46)	9,200
	$30,800

The Long and Short of After-tax Cash Flows

In general, a project's cash flows will fall into one of three categories: (1) the initial investment, (2) the differential flows over the project's life and (3) the terminal cash flow. The capital-budgeting criteria, which were discussed in the previous chapter, will use these cash flows as inputs.

Initial Investment – Incremental Investment

The initial investment involves the immediate cash outlay necessary to purchase the asset and put it in operating order. This amount includes the cost of installing the asset (the asset's purchase price plus any expenses associated with transportation or installation) and any nonexpense cash outlays, such as increased working capital requirements. If we are considering a new sales outlet, there might be additional cash flows associated with investment in working capital in the form of increased inventory and cash necessary to operate the sales outlet. While these cash flows are not included in the cost of the asset or even expensed on the books, they must be included in our analysis.

The after-tax cost of expense items incurred as a result of new investment must also be included as cash outflows—for example, any training expenses or special engineering expenses that would not have been incurred otherwise. Finally, if the investment decision is a replacement decision, the cash inflow associated with the selling price of the old asset, in addition to any tax effects resulting from its sale, must be accounted for.

Items included in the initial outlay calculation are summarized in Table 12.1.

Table 12.1: Initial Investment

1. Purchase price of asset and installation cost
2. Additional expenses on an after-tax basis (for example, training expenses)
3. Additional nonexpense outlays incurred (for example, working capital investments)
4. In a replacement decision, the after-tax cash flow associated with the disposal of the old asset

Tax Effects of Disposal

In general, gains and losses (i.e., the disposal value minus the book value) on disposal of equipment are taxed in the same way as ordinary gains and losses. Immediate disposal of the old equipment results in a loss that is fully tax deductible from current income. The loss (the excess of the book value over the disposal value) must be computed to isolate its effect on current income tax, but the total cash inflow is the sales price plus the current income tax benefit.

In short, there are three possible tax situations dealing with the sale of an old asset:

1. The old asset is sold for a price above the depreciated value is considered recapture of depreciation (or gain) and taxed at the corporate tax rate. If, for example, the old machine was originally purchased for $15,000, had a book (undepreciated) value of $10,000 and was sold for $14,000, assuming the firm's tax rate is 40 percent, the taxes on gain (due from recapture of depreciation) would be ($14,000 - $10,000)(.40), or $1,600. The after- tax cash inflow then is $14,000 - $1,600 = $12,400.
2. The old asset is sold for its depreciated value. In this case no taxes result, as there is neither a gain nor a loss in the asset's sale. The after-tax cash inflow is the selling price (disposal value) - $10,000.
3. The old asset is sold for less than its depreciated value. In this case the difference between the depreciated book value and the salvage value of the asset is used to offset ordinary income and thus results in tax savings. Assume that the machine was sold for $8,000, while its book value is $10,000. Two cash inflows are connected with this sale.
   - A $8,000 cash inflow in the form of the sales price and
   - A $800 cash inflow in the form of a reduction in income taxes,

   resulting from the tax shield provided by the loss sustained on the sale, just like the tax shield provided by depreciation deduction, as computed as follows:

book value		$10,000
selling price		8,000
loss		2,000
tax shield	x .40	$800

Thus, the total cash inflow from the disposal is $8,800 ($8,000 + $800).

Example 6

Assume a company in the 40 percent tax bracket contemplating the purchase of a new machine to be used in oil and gas drilling for $30,000. It has a useful life of five years and will be depreciated using the straight-line method. The new machine will replace an existing machine originally purchased for $30,000, 10 years ago, which currently has five more years of expected useful life. The existing machine will generate $2,000 of depreciation expenses for each of the next five years, at which time the book value will be equal to zero. To put the new machine in running order, it is necessary to pay shipping charges of $2,000 and installation charges of $3,000. Because the new machine will work faster than the old one, it will require and increase in goods-in-process inventory of $3,000. Finally, the old machine can be sold to a scrap dealer for $15,000.

The installed cost of the new machine would be the $30,000 cost plus $2,000 shipping and $3,000 installation fees, for a total of $35,000. Additional outflows are associated with taxes incurred on the sale of the old machine and with increased investment in inventory. Although the old machine has a book value of $10,000, it could be sold for $15,000. The increased taxes on a gain (from recapture of depreciation) will be equal to the sales price of the old machine less its book value times the firm's tax rate, or ($15,000 - $10,000)(.4), or $2,000.

The increase in goods-in-process inventory of $3,000 must also be considered part of the initial outlay, which will be recovered at the termination of the project. In effect, the firm invests $3,000 in inventory now, resulting in an initial cash outlay, and liquidates this inventory in five years, resulting in a $3,000 cash inflow at the end of the project. The total outlays associated with the new machine are $35,000 for its installed cost, $2,000 in increased taxes and $3,000 in investment in inventory, for a total of $40,000. This is somewhat offset by the sale of the old machine for $15,000. Thus, the initial investment associated with this project is $25,000, as shown in Table 12.2.

Table 12.2: Calculation of Initial Investment

Out-of-pocket outlays:	
Installed cost of machine	$35,000
Increased taxes from sale of old machine (15,000-$10,000)(.4)	2,000
Increased investment in inventory	3,000
Total outlays	$40,000
Inflows:	
Salvage value of old machine	15,000
Initial outlay	$25,000

Differential Flows over the Project's Life

The differential cash flows over the project's life involve the incremental after-tax cash flows resulting from increased revenues, plus labor or material savings, and reductions in selling expenses. Any major repair and overhaul costs must be included. Furthermore, an adjustment for the incremental change in taxes should be made, including any increase in taxes that might result from increased profits or any tax savings from an increase in depreciation expenses. Increased depreciation expenses affect tax-related cash flows by reducing taxable income and thus lowering taxes. Table 12.3 lists some of the factors that might be involved in determining a project's differential cash flows.

Table 12.3: Differential Cash Flows on an After-tax Basis

1. Incremental revenue
2. Labor and material savings
3. Increases in overhead or overhaul incurred
4. In a replacement decision depreciation tax shield on an incremental basis

In the example, assume further that purchasing the machine is expected to reduce salaries by $10,000 per year and fringe benefits by $1,000 annually, because it will take only one person to operate, whereas the old machine requires two operators. In addition, the cost of defects will fall from $8,000 per year to $3,000. However, maintenance expenses will increase by $4,000 annually. The annual depreciation on this new machine is $7,000 per year, while the depreciation expense lost with the sale of the old machine is $2,000 for each of the next five years. Annual depreciation on the new machine is calculated using the straight-line method.

Since the depreciation on the old machine is $2,000 per year, the increased depreciation will be from $2,000 per year to $7,000 per year, or an increase of $5,000 per year. Although this increase in depreciation expenses is not a cash flow item, it does affect cash flows by reducing taxable income, which in turn reduces taxes.

To determine the annual net cash flows resulting from the acceptance of this project, the net savings before taxes using both book income and cash flows must be found. The additional taxes are then calculated based upon the before-tax book profit. Table 12.4 shows the determination of the differential cash flows on an after-tax basis. Thus, the differential cash flows over the project's life are $9,200.

Table 12.4: Calculation of Differential Cash Flows

	Book Income	Cash Flow
Savings: Reduced salary	$10,000	$10,000
Reduced fringe benefits	1,000	1,000
Reduced defects ($8,000-$3,000)	5,000	5,000
Costs: Increased maintenance expense	-4,000	-4,000
Increased depreciation expense ($7,000-$2,000)	-5,000	
Net savings before taxes	$7,000	$12,000
Taxes (40%)	-2,800	-2,800
Net cash flow after taxes		$ 9,200
Terminal Cash Flow		

The calculation of the terminal cash flow is much simpler than the preceding two calculations. Flows associated with the project's termination generally include the salvage value of the project plus or minus any taxable gains or losses associated with its sales. In addition to the salvage value, there may be a cash outlay associated with the project termination, such as shutdown costs. Finally, any working capital outlay—inventory investments—required at the initiation of the project will be recovered by liquidating the inventory. Table 5 lists some of the factors that might affect a project's terminal cash flow.

In this example, the depreciated book value and salvage value of the machine both are equal to zero. However, there will be a cash flow associated with the recapture of the initial outlay of work-in-process inventory of $3,000. This flow is generated from the liquidation of the $3,000 investment in work-in-process inventory. Therefore, the expected total terminal cash flow equals $3,000.

In summary, the company would have (1) an initial outlay of $25,000, (2) differential cash flows during years 1 through 5 of $9,200 and (3) a terminal cash flow at the end of year 5 of $3,000.

Table 12.5: Terminal Cash Flow on an After-tax Basis

1. The after-tax salvage value of the project
2. Any cash outlays necessary to terminate the project
3. Recapture of nonexpense outlays required at the project's outset (for example, working capital investments)

Types of Depreciation Methods

We saw that depreciation provided the tax shield in the form of (d)(t). Among the commonly used depreciation methods are straight-line and accelerated methods. The two major accelerated methods are sum-of-the-years'-digits (SYD) and double-declining-balance (DDB).

Straight-Line Method

This is the easiest and most popular method of calculating depreciation. It results in equal periodic depreciation charges. The method is most appropriate when an asset's usage is uniform from period to period, as is the case with furniture. The annual depreciation expense is calculated by using the following formula:

$$\text{Depreciation expense} = \frac{\text{Cost} - \text{salvage value}}{\text{Number of years of useful life}}$$

Example 7

An auto is purchased for $20,000 and has an expected salvage value of $2,000. The auto's estimated life is 8 years. Its annual depreciation is calculated as follows:

$$\text{Depreciation expense} = \frac{\text{Cost} - \text{salvage value}}{\text{Number of years of useful life}}$$

$$= \frac{\$20{,}000 - \$2{,}000}{8 \text{ years}} = \$2{,}250/\text{year}$$

An alternative means of computation is to multiply the depreciable cost ($18,000) by the annual depreciation rate, which is 12.5 percent in this example. The annual rate is calculated by dividing the number of years of useful life into one (1/8 = 12.5%). The result is the same: $18,000 x 12.5% = $2,250.

Sum-of-the-Years'-Digits (SYD) Method

In this method, the number of years of life expectancy is enumerated in reverse order in the numerator, and the denominator is the sum of the digits. For example, if the life expectancy of a machine is 8 years, write the numbers in reverse order: 8, 7, 6, 5, 4, 3, 2, 1. The sum of these digits is 36, or (8 + 7 + 6 + 5 + 4 + 3 + 2 + 1). Thus, the fraction for the first year is 8/36, while the fraction for the last year is 1/36. The sum of the eight fractions equals 36/36, or 1. Therefore, at the end of 8 years, the machine is completely written down to its salvage value.

The following formula may be used to quickly find the sum-of-the-years' digits (S):

$$S = \frac{(N)(N + 1)}{2}$$

where N represents the number of years of expected life.

Example 8

In Example 6, the depreciable cost is $18,000 ($20,000 - $2,000). Using the SYD method, the computation for each year's depreciation expense is:

$$S = \frac{(N)(N-1)}{2} = \frac{8(9)}{2} = 72/2 = 36$$

Year	Fraction	x	Depreciation Amount ($)	=	Depreciation Expense
1	8/36		$18,000		$4,000
2	7/36		18,000		3,500
3	6/36		18,000		3,000
4	5/36		18,000		2,500
5	4/36		18,000		2,000
6	3/36		18,000		1,500
7	2/36		18,000		1,000
8	1/36		18,000		500
Total					$18,000

Double-Declining-Balance (DDB) Method

Under this method, depreciation expense is highest in the earlier years and lower in the later years. First, a depreciation rate is determined by doubling the straight-line rate. For example, if an asset has a life of 10 years, the straight-line rate is 1/10 or 10 percent, and the double-declining rate is 20 percent. Second, depreciation expense is computed by multiplying the rate by the book value of the asset at the beginning of each year. Since book value declines over time, the depreciation expense decreases each successive period.

This method ignores salvage value in the computation. However, the book value of the fixed asset at the end of its useful life cannot be below its salvage value.

Example 9

Assume the data in Example 7. Since the straight-line rate is 12.5 percent (1/8), the double-declining-balance rate is 25 percent (2 x 12.5%). The depreciation expense is computed as follows:

Year	Book Value at Beginning	x	Rate (%)	=	Depreciation Expense	Year-end Book Value
1	$20,000		25%		$5,000	$15,000
2	15,000		25		3,750	11,250
3	11,250		25		2,813	8,437
4	8,437		25		2,109	6,328
5	6,328		25		1,582	4,746
6	4,746		25		1,187	3,559
7	3,559		25		890	2,669
8	2,669		25		667	2,002

Note: If the original estimated salvage value had been $2,100 instead of $2,000, the depreciation expense for the eighth year would have been $569 ($2,669 - $2,100) rather than $667, since the asset cannot be depreciated below its salvage value.

Units of Production Method

Under this method, depreciation varies with output.

$$\text{Depreciation per unit} = \frac{\text{Cost} - \text{salvage value}}{\text{Estimated total units that can be produced in the asset's lifetime}}$$

Depreciation = units of output for year x depreciation per unit

Example 10

The cost of a machine is $11,000 with a salvage value of $1,000. The estimated total units are 5,000. The units produced in the first year are 400.

$$\text{Depreciation per unit} = \frac{\$11{,}000 - \$1{,}000}{5{,}000} = \$2 \text{ per unit}$$

Depreciation in year 1 = 400 units x $2 = $800

Which Method to Use

Of course, over the life of the fixed asset, the total depreciation charge will be the same no matter what depreciation method is used; only the timing of the tax savings will differ. The depreciation method used for financial reporting purposes should be realistic for that type of fixed asset. For example, depreciation on an automobile may be based on mileage. The accelerated methods such as SYD and DDB are advantageous for tax purposes since higher depreciation charges in the earlier years result in less income and thus less taxes. The tax savings may then be invested for a return.

Chapter Summary

Since income taxes could make a difference in the accept or reject decision, tax factors must be taken into account in every decision. Although the traditional depreciation methods still can be used for computing depreciation for book purposes, 1981 saw a new way of computing depreciation deductions for tax purposes. The rule is called the modified accelerated cost recovery system (MACRS). We presented an overview of the traditional depreciation methods and illustrated the use of MACRS.

Table 12.6: Modified Accelerated Cost Recovery System Classification of Assets Property class

Year	3-year	5-year	7-year	10-year	15-year	20-year
1	33.3%	20.0%	14.3%	10.0%	5.0%	3.8%
2	44.5	32.0	24.5	18.0	9.5	7.2
3	14.8a	19.2	17.5	14.4	8.6	6.7
4	7.4	11.5a	12.5	11.5	7.7	6.2
5		11.5	8.9a	9.2	6.9	5.7
6		5.8	8.9	7.4	6.2	5.3
7			8.9	6.6a	5.9a	4.9
8			4.5	6.6	5.9	4.5a
9				6.5	5.9	4.5
10				6.5	5.9	4.5
11				3.3	5.9	4.5
12					5.9	4.5
13					5.9	4.5
14					5.9	4.5
15					5.9	4.5
16					3.0	4.4
17						4.4
18						4.4
19						4.4
20						4.4
21						2.2
Total	100%	100%	100%	100%	100%	100%

a. Denotes the year of changeover to straight-line depreciation.

Table 12.7: MACRS Tables by Property Class

MACRS Property Class & Depreciation Method	Useful Life (ADR Midpoint Life) "a"	Examples of Assets
3-year property 200% declining balance	4 years or less	Most small tools are included; the law specifically excludes autos and light trucks from this property class.
5-year property 200% computers, declining balance	More than 4 years to Less than 10 years	Autos and light trucks, typewriters, copiers, duplicating equipment, heavy general- purpose trucks, and research and experimentation equipment are included.
7-year property 200% and declining balance	10 years or more to less than 16 years	Office furniture and fixtures most items of machinery and equipment used in production are included
10-year property 200% declining balance	16 years or more to less than 20 years	Various machinery and equipment, such as that used in petroleum distilling and refining and in the milling of grain, are included.
15-year property 150% declining balance	20 years or more to less than 25 years	Sewage treatment plants telephone and electrical distribution facilities, and land improvements are included.
20-year property 150% declining balance	25 years or more	Service stations and other real property with an ADR midpoint life of less than 27.5 years are included.
27.5-year property Straight-line	Not applicable	All residential rental property is included
31.5-year property Straight-line	Not applicable	All nonresidential property is included.

"a" The term ADR midpoint life means the "useful life" of an asset in a business sense; the appropriate ADR midpoint lives for assets are designated in the tax Regulations.

Financial Tables

Table 1 Future Value of $1 = T1(i,n)

Periods	4%	6%	8%	10%	12%	14%	20%
1	1.040	1.060	1.080	1.100	1.120	1.140	1.200
2	1.082	1.124	1.166	1.210	1.254	1.300	1.440
3	1.125	1.191	1.260	1.331	1.405	1.482	1.728
4	1.170	1.263	1.361	1.464	1.574	1.689	2.074
5	1.217	1.338	1.469	1.611	1.762	1.925	2.488
6	1.265	1.419	1.587	1.772	1.974	2.195	2.986
7	1.316	1.504	1.714	1.949	2.211	2.502	3.583
8	1.369	1.594	1.851	2.144	2.476	2.853	4.300
9	1.423	1.690	1.999	2.359	2.773	3.252	5.160
10	1.480	1.791	2.159	2.594	3.106	3.707	6.192
11	1.540	1.898	2.332	2.853	3.479	4.226	7.430
12	1.601	2.012	2.518	3.139	3.896	4.818	8.916
13	1.665	2.133	2.720	3.452	4.364	5.492	10.699
14	1.732	2.261	2.937	3.798	4.887	6.261	12.839
15	1.801	2.397	3.172	4.177	5.474	7.138	15.407
16	1.873	2.540	3.426	4.595	6.130	8.137	18.488
17	1.948	2.693	3.700	5.055	6.866	9.277	22.186
18	2.026	2.854	3.996	5.560	7.690	10.575	26.623
19	2.107	3.026	4.316	6.116	8.613	12.056	31.948
20	2.191	3.207	4.661	5.728	9.646	13.743	38.338
30	3.243	5.744	10.063	17.450	29.960	50.950	237.380
40	4.801	10.286	21.725	45.260	93.051	188.880	1469.800

Table 2 Future Value of an Annuity of $1 = T2(i,n)

Periods	4%	6%	8%	10%	12%	14%	20%
1	1.000	1.000	1.000	1.000	1.000	1.000	1.000
2	2.040	2.060	2.080	2.100	2.120	2.140	2.200
3	3.122	3.184	3.246	3.310	3.374	3.440	3.640
4	4.247	4.375	4.506	4.641	4.779	4.921	5.368
5	5.416	5.637	5.867	6.105	6.353	6.610	7.442
6	6.633	6.975	7.336	7.716	8.115	8.536	9.930
7	7.898	8.394	8.923	9.487	10.089	10.730	12.916
8	9.214	9.898	10.637	11.436	12.300	13.233	16.499
9	10.583	11.491	12.488	13.580	14.776	16.085	20.799
10	12.006	13.181	14.487	15.938	17.549	19.337	25.959
11	13.486	14.972	16.646	18.531	20.655	23.045	32.150
12	15.026	16.870	18.977	21.385	24.133	37.271	39.580
13	16.627	18.882	21.495	24.523	28.029	32.089	48.497
14	18.292	21.015	24.215	27.976	32.393	37.581	59.196
15	20.024	23.276	27.152	31.773	37.280	43.842	72.035
16	21.825	25.673	30.324	35.950	42.753	50.980	87.442
17	23.698	28.213	33.750	40.546	48.884	59.118	105.930
18	25.645	30.906	37.450	45.600	55.750	68.394	128.120
19	27.671	33.760	41.446	51.160	63.440	78.969	154.740
20	29.778	36.778	45.762	57.276	75.052	91.025	186.690
30	56.085	79.058	113.283	164.496	241.330	356.790	1181.900
40	95.026	154.762	259.057	442.597	767.090	1342.000	7343.900

*Payments (or receipts) at the *end* of each period.

Table 3 Present Value of $1 = T3(i,n)

PERIODS	3%	4%	5%	6%	7%	8%	10%	12%	14%	16%	18%	20%	22%	24%	25%	26%	28%	30%	40%
1	.9709	.9615	.9524	.9434	.9346	.9259	.9091	.8929	.8772	.8621	.8475	.8333	.8197	.8065	.8000	.7937	.7813	.7692	.7143
2	.9426	.9246	.9070	.8900	.8734	.8573	.8264	.7972	.7695	.7432	.7182	.6944	.6719	.6504	.6400	.6299	.6104	.5917	.5102
3	.9151	.8890	.8638	.8396	.8163	.7938	.7513	.7118	.6750	.6407	.6086	.5787	.5507	.5245	.5120	.4999	.4768	.4552	.3644
4	.8885	.8548	.8227	.7921	.7629	.7350	.6830	.6355	.5921	.5523	.5158	.4823	.4514	.4230	.4096	.3968	.3725	.3501	.2603
5	.8626	.8219	.7835	.7473	.7130	.6806	.6209	.5674	.5194	.4761	.4371	.4019	.3700	.3411	.3277	.3149	.2910	.2693	.1859
6	.8375	.7903	.7462	.7050	.6663	.6302	.5645	.5066	.4556	.4104	.3704	.3349	.3033	.2751	.2621	.2499	.2274	.2072	.1328
7	.8131	.7599	.7107	.6651	.6227	.5835	.5132	.4523	.3996	.3538	.3139	.2791	.2486	.2218	.2097	.1983	.1776	.1594	.0949
8	.7894	.7307	.6768	.6274	.5820	.5403	.4665	.4039	.3506	.3050	.2660	.2326	.2038	.1789	.1678	.1574	.1388	.1226	.0678
9	.7664	.7026	.6446	.5919	.5439	.5002	.4241	.3606	.3075	.2630	.2255	.1938	.1670	.1443	.1342	.1249	.1084	.0943	.0484
10	.7441	.6756	.6139	.5584	.5083	.4632	.3855	.3220	.2697	.2267	.1911	.1615	.1369	.1164	.1074	.0992	.0847	.0725	.0346
11	.7224	.6496	.5847	.5268	.4751	.4289	.3505	.2875	.2366	.1954	.1619	.1346	.1122	.0938	.0859	.0787	.0662	.0558	.0247
12	.7014	.6246	.5568	.4970	.4440	.3971	.3186	.2567	.2076	.1685	.1372	.1122	.0920	.0757	.0687	.0625	.0517	.0429	.0176
13	.6810	.6006	.5303	.4688	.4150	.3677	.2897	.2292	.1821	.1452	.1163	.0935	.0754	.0610	.0550	.0496	.0404	.0330	.0126
14	.6611	.5775	.5051	.4423	.3878	.3405	.2633	.2046	.1597	.1252	.0985	.0779	.0618	.0492	.0440	.0393	.0316	.0254	.0090
15	.6419	.5553	.4810	.4173	.3624	.3152	.2394	.1827	.1401	.1079	.0835	.0649	.0507	.0397	.0352	.0312	.0247	.0195	.0064
16	.6232	.5339	.4581	.3936	.3387	.2919	.2176	.1631	.1229	.0930	.0708	.0541	.0415	.0320	.0281	.0248	.0193	.0150	.0046
17	.6050	.5134	.4363	.3714	.3166	.2703	.1978	.1456	.1078	.0802	.0600	.0451	.0340	.0258	.0225	.0197	.0150	.0116	.0033
18	.5874	.4936	.4155	.3503	.2959	.2502	.1799	.1300	.0946	.0691	.0508	.0376	.0279	.0208	.0180	.0156	.0118	.0089	.0023
19	.5703	.4746	.3957	.3305	.2765	.2317	.1635	.1161	.0829	.0596	.0431	.0313	.0229	.0168	.0144	.0124	.0092	.0068	.0017
20	.5537	.4564	.3769	.3118	.2584	.2145	.1486	.1037	.0728	.0514	.0365	.0261	.0187	.0135	.0115	.0098	.0072	.0053	.0012
21	.5375	.4388	.3589	.2942	.2415	.1987	.1351	.0926	.0638	.0443	.0309	.0217	.0154	.0109	.0092	.0078	.0056	.0040	.0009
22	.5219	.4220	.3418	.2775	.2257	.1839	.1228	.0826	.0560	.0382	.0262	.0181	.0126	.0088	.0074	.0062	.0044	.0031	.0006
23	.5067	.4057	.3256	.2618	.2109	.1703	.1117	.0738	.0491	.0329	.0222	.0151	.0103	.0071	.0059	.0049	.0034	.0024	.0004
24	.4919	.3901	.3101	.2470	.1971	.1577	.1015	.0659	.0431	.0284	.0188	.0126	.0085	.0057	.0047	.0039	.0027	.0018	.0003
25	.4776	.3751	.2953	.2330	.1842	.1460	.0923	.0588	.0378	.0245	.0160	.0105	.0069	.0046	.0038	.0031	.0021	.0014	.0002
26	.4637	.3607	.2812	.2198	.1722	.1352	.0839	.0525	.0331	.0211	.0135	.0087	.0057	.0037	.0030	.0025	.0016	.0011	.0002
27	.4502	.3468	.2678	.2074	.1609	.1252	.0763	.0469	.0291	.0182	.0115	.0073	.0047	.0030	.0024	.0019	.0013	.0008	.0001
28	.4371	.3335	.2551	.1956	.1504	.1159	.0693	.0419	.0255	.0157	.0097	.0061	.0038	.0024	.0019	.0015	.0010	.0006	.0001
29	.4243	.3207	.2429	.1846	.1406	.1073	.0630	.0374	.0224	.0135	.0082	.0051	.0031	.0020	.0015	.0012	.0008	.0005	.0001
30	.4120	.3083	.2314	.1741	.1314	.0994	.0573	.0334	.0196	.0116	.0070	.0042	.0026	.0016	.0012	.0010	.0006	.0004	.0000
40	.3066	.2083	.1420	.0972	.0668	.0460	.0221	.0107	.0053	.0026	.0013	.0007	.0004	.0002	.0001	.0001	.0001	.0000	.0000

Table 4 Present Value of an Annuity of $1 = T4(i,n)

Periods	3%	4%	5%	6%	7%	8%	10%	12%	14%	16%	18%	20%	22%	24%
1	.9709	.9615	.9524	.9434	.9346	.9259	.9091	.8929	.8772	.8621	.8475	.8333	.8197	.8065
2	1.9135	1.8861	1.8594	1.8334	1.8080	1.7833	1.7355	1.6901	1.6467	1.6052	1.5656	1.5278	1.4915	1.4568
3	2.8286	2.7751	2.7232	2.6730	2.6243	2.5771	2.4869	2.4018	2.3216	2.2459	2.1743	2.1065	2.0422	1.9813
4	3.7171	3.6299	3.5460	3.4651	3.3872	3.3121	3.1699	3.0373	2.9137	2.7982	2.6901	2.5887	2.4936	2.4043
5	4.5797	4.4518	4.3295	4.2124	4.1002	3.9927	3.7908	3.6048	3.4331	3.2743	3.1272	2.9906	2.8636	2.7454
6	5.4172	5.2421	5.0757	4.9173	4.7665	4.6229	4.3553	4.1114	3.8887	3.6847	3.4976	3.3255	3.1669	3.0205
7	6.2303	6.0021	5.7864	5.5824	5.3893	5.2064	4.8684	4.5638	4.2883	4.0386	3.8115	3.6046	3.4155	3.2423
8	7.0197	6.7327	6.4632	6.2098	5.9713	5.7466	5.3349	4.9676	4.6389	4.3436	4.0776	3.8372	3.6193	3.4212
9	7.7861	7.4353	7.1078	6.8017	6.5152	6.2469	5.7590	5.3282	4.9464	4.6065	4.3030	4.0310	3.7863	3.5655
10	8.5302	8.1109	7.7217	7.3601	7.0236	6.7101	6.1446	5.6502	5.2161	4.8332	4.4941	4.1925	3.9232	3.6819
11	9.2526	8.7605	8.3064	7.8869	7.4987	7.1390	6.4951	5.9377	5.4527	5.0286	4.6560	4.3271	4.0354	3.7757
12	9.9540	9.3851	8.8633	8.3838	7.9427	7.5361	6.8137	6.1944	5.6603	5.1971	4.7932	4.4392	4.1274	3.8514
13	10.6350	9.9856	9.3936	8.8527	8.3577	7.9038	7.1034	6.4235	5.8424	5.3423	4.9095	4.5327	4.2028	3.9124
14	11.2961	10.5631	9.8986	9.2950	8.7455	8.2442	7.3667	6.6282	6.0021	5.4675	5.0081	4.6106	4.2646	3.9616
15	11.9379	11.1184	10.3797	9.7122	9.1079	8.5595	7.6061	6.8109	6.1422	5.5755	5.0916	4.6755	4.3152	4.0013
16	12.5611	11.6523	10.8378	10.1059	9.4466	8.8514	7.8237	6.9740	6.2651	5.6685	5.1624	4.7296	4.3567	4.0333
17	13.1661	12.1657	11.2741	10.4773	9.7632	9.1216	8.0216	7.1196	6.3729	5.7487	5.2223	4.7746	4.3908	4.0591
18	13.7535	12.6593	11.6896	10.8276	10.0591	9.3719	8.2014	7.2497	6.4674	5.8178	5.2732	4.8122	4.4187	4.0799
19	14.3238	13.1339	12.0853	11.1581	10.3356	9.6036	8.3649	7.3658	6.5504	5.8775	5.3162	4.8435	4.4415	4.0967
20	14.8775	13.5903	12.4622	11.4699	10.5940	9.8181	8.5136	7.4694	6.6231	5.9288	5.3527	4.8696	4.4603	4.1103
21	15.4150	14.0292	12.8212	11.7641	10.8355	10.0168	8.6487	7.5620	6.6870	5.9731	5.3837	4.8913	4.4756	4.1212
22	15.9369	14.4511	13.1630	12.0416	11.0612	10.2007	8.7715	7.6446	6.7429	6.0113	5.4099	4.9094	4.4882	4.1300
23	16.4436	14.8568	13.4886	12.3034	11.2722	10.3711	8.8832	7.7184	6.7921	6.0442	5.4321	4.9245	4.4985	4.1371
24	16.9355	15.2470	13.7986	12.5504	11.4693	10.5288	8.9847	7.7843	6.8351	6.0726	5.4509	4.9371	4.5070	4.1428
25	17.4131	15.6221	14.0939	12.7334	11.6536	10.6748	9.0770	7.8431	6.8729	6.0971	5.4669	4.9476	4.5139	4.1474
26	17.8768	15.9828	14.3752	13.0032	11.8258	10.8100	9.1609	7.8957	6.9061	6.1182	5.4804	4.9563	4.5196	4.1511
27	18.3270	16.3296	14.6430	13.2105	11.9867	10.9352	9.2372	7.9426	6.9352	6.1364	5.4919	4.9636	4.5243	4.1542
28	18.7641	16.6631	14.8981	13.4062	12.1371	11.0511	9.3066	7.9844	6.9607	6.1520	5.5016	4.9697	4.5281	4.1566
29	19.1885	16.9837	15.1411	13.5907	12.2777	11.1584	9.3696	8.0218	6.9830	6.1656	5.5098	4.9747	4.5312	4.1585
30	19.6004	17.2920	15.3725	13.7648	12.4090	11.2578	9.4269	8.0552	7.0027	6.1772	5.5168	4.9789	4.5338	4.1601
40	23.1148	19.7928	17.1591	15.0463	13.3317	11.9246	9.7791	8.2438	7.1050	6.2335	5.5482	4.9966	4.5439	4.1659

Glossary

ABC ANALYSIS inventory control system that divides the inventory into three classes.

ACTIVITY-BASED COSTING (ABC) a costing system which first traces costs to activities and then to products. It separates overhead costs into overhead cost pools, where each cost pool is associated with a different cost driver. A predetermined overhead rate is computed for each cost pool and each cost driver. In consequence, this method has enhanced product costing accuracy.

ACTIVITY-BASED MANAGEMENT (ABM) systemwide, integrated approach that focuses management's attention on activities with the goal of improving customer value, reducing costs, and the resulting profit.

ANALYSIS OF VARIANCES (VARIANCE ANALYSIS) analysis and investigation of causes for variances between standard costs and actual costs. A variance is considered favorable if actual costs are less than standard costs; it is unfavorable if actual costs exceed standard costs. Unfavorable variances are the ones that need further investigation for their causes.

BENCHMARKING searching for new and better procedures by comparing your own procedures to that of the very best.

BREAK-EVEN ANALYSIS a branch of cost-volume-profit (CVP) analysis that determines the break-even sales, which is the level of sales where total costs equal total revenue.

BUSINESS PROCESS REENGINEERING (BPR) approach aiming at making revolutionary changes as opposed to evolutionary changes by eliminating non-value added steps in a business process and computerizing the remaining steps to achieve desired outcomes.

CAPACITY rate at which work is capable of being produced.

CAPITAL BUDGET a budget or plan of proposed acquisitions and replacements of long-term assets and their financing. A capital budget is developed using a variety of capital budgeting techniques such as the discount cash flow method.

CAPITAL RATIONING the problem of selecting the mix of acceptable projects that provides the highest overall net present value (NPV) where a company has a limit on the budget for capital spending.

CASH BUDGET a budget for cash planning and control presenting expected cash inflow and outflow for a designated time period. The cash budget helps management keep cash balances in reasonable relationship to its needs. It aids in avoiding idle cash and possible cash shortages.

CASH FLOW (1) cash receipts minus cash disbursements from a given operation or asset for a given period. Cash flow and cash inflow are often used interchangeably. (2) the monetary value of the expected benefits and costs of a project. It may be in the form of cash savings in operating costs or the difference between additional dollars received and additional dollars paid out for a given period.

COEFFICIENT OF DETERMINATION a statistical measure of how good the estimated regression equation is. Simply put, it is a measure of "goodness of fit" in the regression.

COMMON COSTS expense shared by different departments, products, jobs, also called joint costs or indirect costs.

CONTINUOUS IMPROVEMENT (CI) also called Kaizen in Japanese, never-ending effort for improvement in every part of the firm relative to all of its deliverables to its customers.

CONTRIBUTION MARGIN (CM) the difference between sales and the variable costs of the product or service, also called marginal income. It is the amount of money available to cover fixed costs and generate profits.

CONVERSION COSTS the sum of the costs of direct labor and factory overhead.

CORPORATE BALANCED SCORECARD a set of performance measures constructed for four dimensions of performance. The dimensions are financial, customer, internal processes, and learning and growth.

COST ACCUMULATION the collection of costs in an organized fashion by means of a cost accounting system. There are two primary approaches to cost accumulation: a job order system and process cost system.

COST BEHAVIOR ANALYSIS analysis of mixed costs. Mixed costs must be separated into the variable and fixed elements in order to be included in a variety of business planning analyses such as cost-volume-profit (CVP) analysis.

COST CENTER the unit within the organization in which the manager is responsible only for costs. A cost center has no control over sales or over the generating of revenue. An example is the production department of a manufacturing company.

COST DRIVER a factor that causes a cost item to be incurred (e.g., direct labor hours, number of setups, or number of inspections).

COST MANAGEMENT a system that measures the cost of significant activities, recognizes non-value-added costs, and identifies activities that will improve overall performance.

COST OF PRODUCTION REPORT a summary of the unit and cost data of a production department in a process cost system.

COST POOL a group of related costs that are assigned together to a set of cost objectives (such as jobs, products, or activities).

COST-VOLUME FORMULA a cost function in the form of $y = a + bx$. For example, the cost-volume formula for factory overhead is $y = \$200 + \$10x$ where y = estimated factory overhead and x = direct labor hours, which means that the factory overhead is estimated to be $200 fixed, plus $10 per hour of direct labor. Cost analysts use the formula for cost prediction and flexible budgeting purposes.

COST-VOLUME-PROFIT (CVP) ANALYSIS analysis that deals with how profits and costs change with a change in volume. It looks at the effects on profits of changes in such factors as variable costs, fixed costs, selling prices, volume, and mix of products sold.

DEPARTMENTAL RATE a predetermined factory overhead rate for each production department.

DISCRETIONARY (FIXED) COSTS those fixed costs that change because of managerial decisions, also called management (fixed) costs or programmed (fixed) costs. Examples of this type of fixed costs are advertising outlays, training costs, and research and development costs.

DO PONT FORMULA the breakdown of return on investment (ROL) into profit margin and asset turnover.

FLEXIBLE BUDGET a budget based on cost-volume relationships and developed for the actual level of activity. An extremely useful tool for comparing the actual cost incurred to the cost allowable for the activity level achieved.

INTERNAL RATE OF RETURN (IRR) the rate of interest that equates the initial investment with the present value of future cash inflows.

INVESTMENT CENTER a responsibility center within an organization that has control over revenue, cost, and investment funds. It is a profit center whose performance is evaluated on the basis of the return earned on invested capital.

JOB ORDER COSTING the accumulation of costs by specific jobs, contracts, or orders. This costing method is appropriate when direct costs can be identified with specific units of production. Widely used by custom manufacturers such as printing, aircraft, construction, auto repair, and professional services.

JUST-IN-TIME (JIT) a demand-pull system where demand for customer output (not plans for using input resources) triggers production. Production activities are "pulled," not "pushed," into

action. JIT, in its purest sense, is buying and producing in very small quantities just in time for use.

JUST-IN-TIME PRODUCTION approach to manufacturing in which items are produced only when needed in production.

KANBAN Japanese information system for coordinating production orders and withdrawals from in-process inventory to realize just-in-time production.

LABOR EFFICIENCY VARIANCE the difference between the amount of labor time that should have been used and the labor actually used, multiplied by the standard rate.

LABOR RATE VARIANCE any deviation from standard in the average hourly rate paid to workers.

LEAST SQUARES METHOD a statistical technique for fitting a straight line through a set of points in such a way that the sum of the squared distances from the data points to the line is minimized.

MASTER (COMPREHENSIVE) BUDGET a plan of activities expressed in monetary terms of the assets, equities, revenues, and costs which will be involved in carrying out the plans. A set of projected or planned financial statements.

MATERIALS PRICE VARIANCE the difference between what is paid for a given quantity of materials and what should have been paid, multiplied by actual quantity of materials purchased.

MATERIALS QUANTITY (USAGE) VARIANCE the difference between the actual quantity of materials used in production and the standard quantity of materials allowed for actual production, multiplied by the standard price per unit.

MIXED COSTS costs that vary with changes in volume but, unlike variable costs, do not vary in direct proportion, also called semi-variable costs.

MULTIPLE REGRESSION ANALYSIS a statistical procedure that attempts to assess the relationship between the dependent variable and two or more independent variables. For example, total factory overhead is related to both labor hours and machine hours.

NET PRESENT VALUE (NPV) the difference between the present value of cash inflows generated by the project and the amount of the initial investment.

OPPORTUNITY COST the net benefit foregone by rejecting an alternative use of time or facilities.

OUT-OF-POCKET COSTS actual cash outlays made during the period for payroll, advertising, and other operating expenses.

PAYBACK PERIOD the length of time required to recover the initial amount of a capital investment.

PREDETERMINED OVERHEAD RATE an overhead rate, based on budgeted factory overhead cost and budgeted activity, which is established before a period begins.

PROCESS COSTING a cost accumulation method used to assign costs to units of a homogeneous product as the units pass through one or more processes.

PROFIT-VOLUME CHART a chart that determines how profits vary with changes in volume.

PROFITABILITY INDEX the ratio of the total present value of future cash inflows to the initial investment.

RATE OF RETURN ON INVESTMENT (ROI) (1) for the company as a whole, net income after taxes divided by invested capital. (2) for the segment of an organization, net operating income divided by operating assets, (3) for capital budgeting purposes. also called simple accounting, or unadjusted rate of return, expected future net income divided by initial (or average) investment.

REGRESSION ANALYSIS a statistical procedure for mathematically estimating the average relationship between the dependent variable (sales, for example) and one or more independent variables (price and advertising, for example).

RELEVANT COST the expected future cost that will differ between the alternatives being considered.

RESIDUAL INCOME (RI) the operating income which an investment center is able to earn above some minimum return on its assets.

RESPONSIBILITY ACCOUNTING the collection, summarization, and reporting of financial information about various decision centers (responsibility centers) throughout an organization. Also called activity accounting or profitability accounting.

RESPONSIBILITY CENTER a unit in the organization which has control over costs, revenues, or investment funds. For accounting purposes, responsibility centers are classified as cost centers, revenue centers, profit centers, and investment centers, depending on what each center is responsible for.

SEGMENTED REPORTING the process of reporting activities of various segments of an organization such as divisions, product lines, or sales territories.

SHADOW PRICE profit that would be lost by not adding an additional hour of capacity.

SIMPLE REGRESSION a regression analysis which involves one independent variable. For example, total factory overhead is related to one activity variable (either direct labor hours or machine hours).

THEORY OF CONSTRAINTS (TOC) approach seeking to identify a company's constraints or bottlenecks and exploit them so that throughput is maximized and inventories and operating costs are minimized.

TOTAL QUALITY MANAGEMENT (TQM) concept of using quality methods and techniques to strategic advantage within firms.

VARIANCE (1) in statistics, the square of the standard deviation, (2) in cost analysis, the deviation between the actual cost and the standard cost.

VOLUME-BASED COST DRIVER a cost driver that is based on production volume, such as machine hours or direct-labor hours.

ZERO-BASE BUDGETING a method of budgeting in which cost and benefit estimates are built up from scratch, from the level of zero, and must be justified.

Index

D

E

F

H

I

J

L

M

N

O

P